The Who

and the making of
TOMMY

The Who

and the making of
TOMMY

NIGEL CAWTHORNE

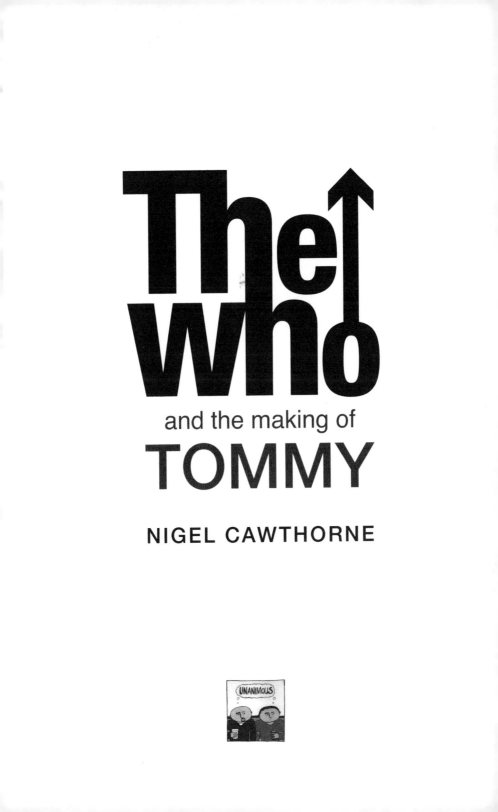

The publisher wishes to thank the Book Division at Lasgo Chrysalis London for their ongoing support in developing this series.

Published by Unanimous Ltd
Unanimous Ltd. is an imprint of MQ Publications Ltd.
12 The Ivories, 6–8 Northampton Street, London, N1 2HY

Printed and bound in France

ISBN: 1 90331 876 9

1 2 3 4 5 6 7 8 9

Picture credits:
Cover: John Fowler/Rex Features.
Picture section page 1: © Harry Goodwin/Redferns; pages 2–3: Rex Features; page 2 bottom: Peter Sanders/Rex Features; page 4 (both): © Baron Wolman, www.baronwolman.com; page 5 top: Private collection, USA, www.thewho.info; page 5 bottom: © Fortean/TopFoto.co.uk; page 6: © Henry Diltz/Corbis; page 7: Private collection, USA, www.thewho.info; page 8 top: © Robert Stigwood Productions/Columbia TriStar/Getty Images; page 8 bottom: Nils Jorgensen/Rex Features.

contents

introduction

As an album, *Tommy* is unique. Made by a band famous for their singles in the 1960s—not to mention trashing hotel rooms, smashing their equipment on stage, and putting a Rolls-Royce in a swimming pool—*Tommy* was a fully fledged "rock opera." Some have argued that, if a classical analogy is needed, it is more accurate to say that it is a rock cantata— that is, a piece that is sung through, rather than sung and acted. Nevertheless, it had an operatic structure with an overture, musical coherence, a defined plot line, and distinct characters. Added to that it had philosophical and religious underpinnings, an element of mysticism, and roots firmly embedded in popular culture.

Tommy did not have the lush strings and full orchestration of other concept albums of the time. It was made to be played on stage by a four-piece rock band. The Who's legendary high-energy stage act lent it a drama that rivaled anything from Verdi, Puccini, Debussy, or Wagner. And, like a proper opera should be performed, The Who played the whole of *Tommy* through without a break.

In the late 1960s and early 1970s *Tommy* was played in opera houses as well as large stadiums and rock venues. The Who were the first and last rock band to play New York's Metropolitan Opera House—the largest opera house in the world. In all the band played *Tommy* more than 160 times on stage.

In 1972, three years after the album was released, an all-star fully orchestrated version came out. This, too, took to the stage. Ballet versions and fully walked-through opera versions appeared across North America. In 1975, there was a movie version, whose sound track entered the charts. Then in 1993, a musical version hit Broadway. This production toured the world. No other rock album has ever appeared in so many incarnations.

But *Tommy* remained at its core a rock album. No matter how many times The Who tried to drop it from their repertoire, their fans insisted that they play it.

It was said at the time that The Who made *Tommy* and *Tommy* made The Who. This is undoubtedly true. It plucked them from the verge of bankruptcy and made each member of the band a millionaire.

There will never be another band like The Who and there will never be another album like *Tommy*. This is the story of how it was made.

on the skids

The Who were in trouble in 1969, the year *Tommy* came out. It had been four years since "My Generation" had established them as one of Britain's top pop bands. Although the "British invasion" of the U.S. music scene had started the year before "My Generation" was released in 1965, the single had only gone to number 74 in the *Billboard* Hot 100. The following year, they had fallen out with their producer Shel Talmy and, after taking an action in the High Court in England, he had secured five per cent of their record earnings for the next five years—although no one expected any band to last that long.

This made them reluctant to record. Unfortunately, as a stage act, they famously always smashed their equipment, so when touring they barely broke even. Pete Townshend got through 70 guitars a year and complained that he could not even put them down as a deductible expense because the tax man did not believe him. Despite having six top five U.K. singles, by 1969, The Who were an estimated £1,300,000 ($2,000,000) in debt.

In the U.S., they were handled by Decca, who took little interest in their career. And in the U.K., they were not even on a well-known label. They had started out on Brunswick, then moved to Robert Stigwood's Reaction. But in 1967, after spending six weeks studying the production methods of biscuit companies and washing-powder manufacturers—and those of any firm that marketed goods roughly the size of a box of records—The Who's managers, former movie-makers

Kit Lambert and Chris Stamp, started their own record label, Track Records. The Who found themselves almost by default on their managers' new label. This gave the band another new problem. Track immediately signed legend Jimi Hendrix, who had just arrived in the U.K. Up until then, Townshend had been the wild ax man of rock and roll who had introduced the use of feedback and distortion. Now the flamboyant Hendrix, with his technical ability and eccentric playing style, was taking over.

"Hendrix was the first man to walk all over my territory," said Townshend. "I felt incredibly intimidated by that."

While Townshend merely smashed his guitar to pieces in the time-honored fashion, as he had been doing since 1963, Hendrix set fire to his. What's more, The Who were a Mod band, associated with the sharp fashions and op-art styles of the early 1960s. They looked out of place in the new psychedelic, hippie gear. Hendrix looked the business. He rapidly upstaged them.

The year 1968 had started badly with a disastrous tour of Australia with another English band, the Small Faces. Before they even arrived, the Australian press was howling about foreign artists draining money from the Australian economy. The moment The Who reached Sydney, New South Wales, the jet-lagged band-members were herded into a hostile press conference and were, to say the least, uncooperative.

Although the promoter had spent more than $10,000 on equipment, he had failed to buy any decent microphones and Australian P.A.s were not up to handling the level of din The Who produced, rendering the band's strident sound muffled and muddy.

At a stadium show in Sydney, the revolving stage refused to revolve because of the sheer weight of equipment stacked on it. This gave much of the audience at the first show a drastically restricted view. They were allowed to stay on for the second show, but still the stage would not turn. The next night, the police were called in after both The Who and the Small Faces were accused of using obscene language on stage.

A show in Adelaide, South Australia, was delayed for an hour while Townshend searched for a replacement guitar. On January 28, they were thrown off a flight to Sydney. The air hostess had refused to serve them and an off-duty pilot accused them of being drunk and using foul language. The plane was then diverted to Melbourne, Victoria, where they were greeted by ranks of State and Commonwealth police who escorted them off the plane.

Accused of "behaving in such a manner as to constitute a risk to the aircraft," they were held for three hours in the V.I.P. lounge after the pilot of a connecting flight to Sydney refused to carry them. After giving assurances of good behavior, The Who were allowed to board a chartered flight, accompanied by four officers of the Department of Civil Aviation.

As they left for New Zealand, the state premier of Victoria, Sir Henry Bolte, told the press that they were, "a mob of crummy hooligans." Townshend vowed never to set foot in Australia again. He never has.

But things were little better in New Zealand.

At the 6 p.m. show at the Town Hall in Auckland on the North Island, they found that an inferior P.A. system had been provided. After the early show, they headed back to the hotel in a rage and threatened to pull out of the second show unless something was done about it. The 8.30 show was delayed until 9.15 while replacement microphones were found. Roger Daltrey, then took great delight in smashing seven of them. The evening ended with a well-publicized riot at the 21st birthday party of the Small Faces' guitarist and singer Steve Marriott at the city's Waterloo Hotel.

After The Who and the Small Faces had flown out, the mass-circulation New Zealand newspaper *The Truth* condemned them as "the scruffiest bunch of Poms that ever milked money from this country's kids... they took nearly 8,000 kids for $2.60 and $3.60 each." And a British émigré complained, "They did more to harm the British image than [1960s U.K. prime ministers] Harold Wilson or Edward Heath could do in ten years. I'm ashamed to have come from the same country as these unwashed, foul-mouthed, booze-swilling no-hopers. Britain can have them."

It is true that, by 1968, The Who were making an impression in the U.S. and Canada and had become the fourth biggest draw behind Cream, the Jimi Hendrix Experience and the Doors. But that was not helping. They needed hit records to survive.

"It's all right on stage and the audiences are quite incredible," Townshend told *Disc* magazine. "But you just keep slogging away, traveling the highways and the freeways and the byways and the airways... You can't work, you can't think—your mind's blanked out."

And there was no respite in sight. With the single exception of "I Can See For Miles"—which reached number nine in the *Billboard* chart on November 25, 1967—none of their singles had reached the top 20. And "Call Me

Lightning," released while the band were touring the U.S. in May 1968, peaked at number 40. It was not even released in the U.K. The record had been withdrawn because the band felt that it was "unrepresentative of our current sound."

"I Can See For Miles" reached number ten in the U.K. In June 1968, they released "Dogs," which peaked at 25. Townshend blamed the B.B.C. The Who and the other British rock bands of the early 1960s had come to fame through the pirate radio stations that broadcast pop music from ships moored outside the U.K.'s territorial waters. These were banned by the Marine Broadcasting Act of 1967 and Britain's national broadcasting system, the B.B.C., started Radio One as a home for pop music.

Although it took on many of the D.J.s from the commercial pirate stations, Radio One limited their play lists and bands like The Who suffered. In an interview in the rock magazine, *New Musical Express*, Pete Townshend complained even Steppenwolf's "Born to be Wild" was being denied airplay. He was angry that, as a consequence of the B.B.C.'s conservative policy, The Who had had to release "Dogs"—"because we knew that they could pass it as fit for human consumption." Reminiscent of the Small Faces' "Lazy Sunday," "Dogs" was about a visit to the greyhound race track in White City, west London, and consequently a little parochial. Also the cockney lilt Daltrey adopted on the single would have been incomprehensible in the U.S., so it was never released in the States.

They were doing little better with albums. *The Who Sell Out*, released in November 1967, had only reached number 13 in the U.K. album charts—compared to five for *My Generation* in 1965 and four for *A Quick One* in 1966. *A Quick*

One was released as *Happy Jack* in the U.S. where it reached number 67. *The Who Sell Out* only made number 48 after New York's number one pop station banned it when the station's music director dismissed the album as "disgusting."

The money they could command for gigs in the U.K. plummeted. They were soon reduced to playing universities for as little as £50 ($75) a night. But they were so deep in debt they could not refuse.

"The English scene for us, unfortunately, doesn't compare with America," Townshend told *Melody Maker*. "The States offers us more money, fans, and excitement."

This did not help. Although they were doing well as a touring band in the U.S., they needed to break through in the charts. And Townshend was fresh out of ideas. He considered himself "written out," at least as far as the three-minute single was concerned. But Kit Lambert insisted that they try to cash in on their touring success. He forced them into the studio to record "Magic Bus," which Townshend had written back in 1965, around the same time as "My Generation."

Although Townshend later said that "Magic Bus" was the song he most enjoyed playing on stage, none of them wanted to record it. They got drunk one lunchtime and, with a couple of friends, went into the studio. With John Entwistle's "Dr. Jekyll and Mr. Hyde" on the B-side, it made number 26 in the U.K. and with Entwistle's "Someone's Coming" on the B-side, it climbed to 25 in the U.S.

The Who's U.S. record company, Decca, were getting desperate. Rummaging through the band's back catalog, they put out the album *Magic Bus: The Who on Tour*—giving it a title that made it sound deceptively like a live album although it was, in fact, a compilation of earlier studio work.

The Who had unwittingly colluded in this. When the idea of repackaging some of their early material had come up, the band had given their approval. They had suggested that Decca put out a collection of their early singles that had either been overlooked or were long since unavailable in the U.S., jokingly dubbing it *The Who's Greatest Flops*. But *Magic Bus* was, in fact, a mish-mash of singles, E.P. (extended play) tracks and B-sides—and badly produced to boot. Released in September 1968, the album stalled at 39 and spent just ten weeks in the *Billboard* chart.

The release of *Magic Bus: The Who on Tour* was the, "culmination of all the most terrible things American record companies ever get up to," railed Townshend. "Plus the fact that they made it look like a live album. I mean, that's the worst thing that's ever gone down, and there are a few people in the L.A. part of Decca that I won't even look at, because they were there at the photo sessions, knowing it was for the album cover."

In the U.K., a well-produced compilation album, *Direct Hits*, came out. But this was not definitive either because Track had no access to the tracks produced by Shel Talmy for Brunswick. The U.K. record-buying public had heard it all before—and recently. The album failed to chart. Things were on the slide. The Who needed a hit—and a big one—otherwise they would simply collapse under the weight of their mounting debts.

Despite the band's dire prospects, Townshend was curiously optimistic. The Beatles and others had recently pioneered the idea of the "concept album," where all the tracks related to a single central theme. But Townshend thought he could take the idea further. He believed that he could write an album where the tracks linked one after another into a storyline, so that together they formed a single continuous piece.

True, since 1967 he had been talking about writing a "rock opera." And that's what everybody thought he was doing, just talking. But he had been writing fragments and toying with a narrative to what he initially called *Amazing Journey*. By 1968 it had become *Deaf, Dumb and Blind Boy*. In September, The Who went into the studio with Townshend's notes. They spent eight weeks and £40,000 ($60,000) recording. This was considered an immensely long time and a huge amount of money in the 1960s.

The album was supposed to have been out for Christmas, but Townshend played around with it for another five months. Over that time, it went through another couple of changes of title. Then when it was finally released as a double album simply named *Tommy* in May 1969, it was make-or-break time for The Who.

the rock opera

In the early 1960s, bands made singles. They were played on jukeboxes in cafes and bars, got airplay, and, if the band was lucky, people went out and bought them. Later, when a band had established a back catalog, this would be exploited by reissuing a compilation of songs on an L.P. (long-playing record) with little new material.

The Beach Boys were the first pop group to realize that the L.P., or album, afforded other possibilities. It was possible to link all the tracks to a single theme, so that the album became a distinct entity in itself, rather than just a collection of disparate songs. In 1963, they release *Little Deuce Coupe* with 12 tracks, each about American automobile culture. Then in 1966, Frank Zappa & the Mothers of Invention produced a satire on the world of pop music, called *Freak Out!*

The Beach Boys were working on another fully developed concept album, *SMILE*, but had to abandon it in early 1967 when Brian Wilson slipped into a void of drink and drugs. A number of songs—"Surf's Up," "Good Vibrations," "Cabinessence," and "Heroes and Villains"—appeared on other albums. *SMILE* itself had to wait until the fall of 2004 to see the light of day in a series of concerts and a solo album by Brian Wilson. In it, tracks segue into one another, producing suites. These were bunched around themes such as the elements and European culture's westward expansion to the Americas.

That same year, 1967, the Beatles began work on *Sgt. Pepper's Lonely Hearts Club Band*, which is popularly considered to be the first concept album. On it, each band member was supposed to have adopted a fictional persona as one of the Lonely Hearts Club Band—while a song of that name opens and closes the album. Although "Lonely Hearts Club Band" provided the album with "bookends," most of the songs are unrelated to the central theme and, after Ringo had introduced himself as "Billy Shears" in the first track "A Little Help From My Friends," the idea of adopting fictional characters was abandoned. However, the album retains many of its narrative elements. "Lovely Rita" and "When I'm Sixty-Four" were developed as thorough character sketches and "A Day in the Life" and "She's Leaving Home" were presented as musical short stories.

Also in 1967, the Moody Blues released *Days of Future Passed*. The album traced "everyman's day" from waking in the morning to going to sleep again at night and was tied together musically by the orchestral interludes provided by the London Festival Orchestra, a group of classical musicians hastily thrown together for the session. The Moody Blues had originally intended to produce a rock version of Dvořák's *New World Symphony*, which explains its musical unity. They abandoned that idea and then—ironically in the light of what happened with *Tommy*—tried to produce an album based on a stage show they were working on.

Until 1967, the Moody Blues were known as an R&B band. They faced opposition from the executives at their label, Deram Records, who felt *Days of Future Passed* might alienate rock fans without bringing new sales from the devotees of classical music. They were wrong. The album went gold in 1970 and continued to surface in the album charts right up to 1973. Its references to drug use and the hallucinogenic feel of the album were perfectly in tune with the times in which it was made.

After the success of *Days of Future Passed*, the concept album then became the province of progressive rock. King Crimson pushed it further by relating their first four albums—*In the Court of King Crimson*, *In the Wake of Poseidon*, *Lizard* and *Island*—to the four Classical elements—air, water, fire, and earth. Pete Townshend described *In the Court of King Crimson*, released the same year as *Tommy*, as "an uncanny masterpiece." But the psychedelic output of the progressive rockers never achieved—or even attempted—the narrative coherence of *Tommy*.

Other British bands followed the Beatles' lead, putting together songs on a related theme to form a song cycle on vinyl. The Small Faces produced *Ogden's Nut Gone Flake*, the Kinks *The Village Green Preservation Society*, and the Pretty Things *S.F. Sorrow*—which is said to be the first true "rock opera." But it was no threat. It failed to chart in the U.K. and the Pretty Things were unknown in the U.S.

Townshend conceded, "Their approach was exactly the same, and it was a natural evolution for rock at the time."

Even so Townshend can claim to have beaten the Pretty Things to it. In 1966, The Who's second album, called *A Quick One* in the U.K. and *Happy Jack* in the U.S., came up short, so Kit Lambert, who was producing the album as well as managing the band, told Townshend to write a long song to conclude the album. Townshend thought that this was a contradiction in terms as, in his view, "rock songs are three minutes 50 by definition." Instead, he linked together four three-minute songs and other fragments. Together they told the story of a woman trying to get laid after her husband had gone missing. Townshend jokingly called them a "mini-opera" and they appeared on the album under the title "A Quick One While He's Away."

A Quick One even came out six months before the Beatles released *Sgt. Pepper.* It may not have helped their finances much, but it secured The Who's reputation as being one of the most innovative rock groups around.

However, just as Townshend began to talk about writing a full-blown "rock opera," he found that there was another contender. In 1967, Keith West of the British psychedelic group Tomorrow announced that he was working on a *Teenage Opera*, and he released two singles from it—"Excerpt from a Teenage Opera" and "Sam."

"Excerpt from a Teenage Opera" made number two in the U.K. charts in August 1967. The follow-up "Sam" only made it to number 38 in November. It seemed that someone had stolen Townshend's thunder and, as "Sam" had done so badly, he began to wonder whether West had not killed the idea of a rock opera completely.

the writer of **Tommy**

The making of the album *Tommy* was a collaborative effort. Every member of The Who lent a shoulder to the wheel. And it certainly would not have happened without Kit Lambert. The son of the composer and conductor, Constance Lambert, he had a background in classical music and constantly urged Pete Townshend to stretch himself.

But it was Townshend who wrote *Tommy*. It was his brainchild and without his towering genius *Tommy*—the album, the opera, the movie, and the musical—would never have happened. When he wrote it, he thought that it was an allegory of what was going on in the 1960s. But 25 years on he came to realize that it was, in fact, "completely autobiographical."

Peter Dennis Blandford Townshend was born on May 19, 1945—just ten days after the end of World War II in Europe—at Nazareth House, a convent annexed as a wartime maternity ward by the nearby West Middlesex Hospital in the western reaches of London, England. There was musical talent on both sides of his family. His father played the alto sax and got star billing on the pre-war music halls as "Cliff Townshend and His Singing Saxophone" and Pete's paternal grandfather, Horace, played the flute and the piccolo in the Jack Shepard Concert Review.

Under her maiden name, Betty Dennis, Pete's mother was a singer and in the 1930s was the featured vocalist with both the Sidney Torch Orchestra and the Les Dennis Orchestra. Her father was a singer with the Black and White Minstrels, a singing troupe in which the men blacked up, and her mother was a well-known vocalist and comedienne.

During World War II, Cliff joined in the Royal Air Force's wartime dance band, which went on to become Britain's most popular show band, the Squadronaires. When the singer got sick, Betty, who had also joined the R.A.F., covered for her on Sundays. She and Cliff then had a whirlwind romance and after seven weeks—that is, seven Sundays—they got married.

After the war, Cliff stayed on with the band and, at the age of just 13 months, Pete saw his father perform during a summer season at Butlin's Holiday Camp in the east-coast resort of Clacton-on-Sea, Essex. Of course, in *Tommy*, Tommy sets up a holiday camp for his followers, although Townshend said this was Keith Moon's idea.

The family moved into a large house in Woodgrange Avenue, off Ealing Common in west London, but his parents were away a lot, touring clubs and military bases all over Europe and he was left in the care of Betty's family.

"I was alone often," he said, "and remember waiting, but I was always sure they would come."

He saw his parents mostly on seaside vacations when they were playing English coastal resorts. One of his most poignant memories of childhood was being on the dunes at the northern resort of Filey, Yorkshire, when he was about two, and watching his parents riding off down the beach laughing and waving. They were only gone a few minutes—his mother did not even recall the event—but he felt abandoned. The feeling stayed with him. Years later, he said, "I grew up with parents who came out of the end of the war with a great resilience, excitement, and big ideas, and I got a bit left behind."

On these vacations, Pete also got to see his parents perform numbers by Glenn Miller and Benny Goodman for the people on vacation. Throughout his life he has always loved the big-band music he heard his parents play, and he has always admired the craftsmanship of the songwriters George Gershwin, Cole Porter, and Johnny Mercer.

These vacations also provided the impulse to make music himself. On trip to the Isle of Man, in the Irish Sea east of Northern Ireland, he met a performing Texan cowboy who promised him a harmonica. Pete never got it and, a couple of years later, resorted to stealing one from a shop.

Like many wartime marriages, the Townshends' began to give at the seams when the conflict was over and after three years Cliff and Betty split up. Pete was sent to live with his grandmother in Kent. "Granny Denny," as he called her, had been deserted by a wealthy lover and, now, in her fifties, was going slowly insane.

"She ran naked in the streets and stuff like that," said Townshend. "She was completely nuts."

She was also very strict and Pete hated her. He longed to have his parents back and two years passed before his mother and father realized they had left Pete with someone who was going mad. Granny Denny would take him out on expeditions to find old handkerchiefs and other bits of rubbish she could re-use or sell. One day, Pete found a pound note on the ground. Granny Denny grabbed it, saying that after it had been boiled it would be as good as new.

Often she would go out at night, leaving Pete on his own. Sometimes he would wake crying in an empty house. Things were no better if she was home. Fearing for his safety, the four-year-old Pete would lock his bedroom door. Townshend said that was where the refrain "see me, feel me, touch me" came from. The eponymous hero of *Tommy*, Townshend realized in later life, was the young Pete himself.

Much of what happened in Granny Denny's house was blanked from Townshend's mind. Years later he recalled, "There was a period of darkness in my life; a bit that I don't remember. My mom and dad split up for a while. Now this is not something I knew when I wrote *Tommy*. It's only something that I found out recently... But in a sense it amounted to me to a kind of abuse because the person that they farmed me out to was my mother's mother who turned out to be clinically insane."

When he was making the movie of *Tommy*, director Ken Russell realized that there were huge holes in the plot.

"It's almost as though the album started almost halfway through the story," he said. "The first half was in his mind but had never been written."

The first half, perhaps, occurred in Granny Denny's house in Kent. However, there are clues. In the album, the defenseless Tommy does suffer at the hands of his family. Granny Denny, it seems, became transmuted into Uncle Ernie, who interferes with him sexually, and Cousin Kevin, who physically abuses him. The autistic Tommy also spends his time staring into a mirror—exactly the sort of thing a young child alone in a house would do.

Ken Russell also pointed out, "You never knew exactly who the father was, why the father was killed or why the boy went blind, deaf, and dumb."

The album starts in World War I, when Tommy's mother, Mrs. Walker, hears that her husband, Captain Walker, is missing in action. She takes a lover. In 1921, Captain Walker returns, finds his wife with her lover and kills him, while Tommy watches the incident in the mirror. It is their anger at Tommy for witnessing the event that propels him into autism.

It seems that Pete had witnessed something similarly traumatic around the same age. In 1991, Townshend had broken his arm and was recuperating at his mother's, when he took the opportunity to ask her what had happened to him between the ages of four and six. She was working on her autobiography at the time and filled in a few of the blanks.

"It didn't contain the kind of trauma Tommy went through," said Townshend, "seeing his mother's lover shot by his father, but it was pretty damn close."

With Cliff Townshend away along on the road with Squadronaires, Pete really did not know much about him. Meanwhile Pete's mother had a number of affairs. The child was often used a "bait" in these tawdry encounters. Townshend remembers his mother pushing him up at steep hill in his pedal car, playing the damsel in distress, so that a man would come to the rescue. The two would then meet again in a coffee bar and the affair blossom. None of this was hidden from Townshend who, like any child, would like to snuggle up with the grown-ups.

"I would be drawn into this tremendous deceit," said Townshend. "When I saw my father, I would feel guilty because I'd been in bed with my mother and her lover."

Despite this, Pete's parents stayed together after he returned from Granny Denny's. But that did not put an end to Pete's troubles. He did not feel that the love he felt for his mother was reciprocated. She was a beautiful woman and his father was a good-looking man. But Pete grew into a pretty ordinary-looking boy and he sensed her disappointment.

"I felt I had something to prove to her," he said. "So in the end I decided that, because I couldn't change the way I looked, I would become a millionaire."

As a lonely child, Townshend became a voracious reader and at the age of seven decided that he wanted to be a journalist when he grew up. In the songs he wrote later, he was certainly an acute observer of the contemporary scene. But his ambition would change. He began to go on the road with his parents. He would watch his father writing arrangements in the tour bus and he later said that he got into music because he had seen his father getting drunk and having a good time while he was working.

Pete got his introduction to show business by being backstage while his father's band was playing. He also heard his mother on record and it was a disappointment to him when his mother gave up singing to run an antiques store on Ealing Common. She settled down and had two more kids. But the way ahead was already set for Townshend.

In the summer of 1956, when the Squadronaires were playing the Isle of Man, Pete's father took him and a childhood friend, Graham "Jumpy" Beard, to the Saturday morning show at the Gaiety Theatre cinema in the island's capital, Douglas. The movie showing was *Rock Around The Clock*, featuring Bill Haley and the Comets, the Platters and the legendary rock-and-roll D.J., Alan Freed.

"*Rock Around the Clock* did it for me," said Townshend. "I hadn't been into rock and roll before that."

At his west London junior school in South Acton, Pete

had sung in the choir and his aunt had encouraged him to play the piano. But after seeing Bill Haley and the Comets, he took up the saxophone. Traditionally part of the line-up of early rock-and-roll bands, saxophones were readily available in the Townshend home. But Townshend was not physically strong. Blowing the sax simply made him go red in the face, so his father suggested that he try his own second instrument, the guitar. Granny Denny bought him one for Christmas when he was 12. But he was woefully inadequate. After a year struggling to learn it, he gave up and switched to the five-stringed banjo to join the traditional—or "trad."—jazz revival that was going on in Britain at the time.

At Acton County Grammar School, Pete joined a trad. band called the Confederates, with a boy named John Entwistle. Born on October 9, 1944, Entwistle was a little older than Townshend. He was an only child whose parents split up when he was just 18 months old. His father, who had been in the Royal Navy during the war, taught him the trumpet, which he in played in the Boys' Brigade—a rival organization to the Boy Scouts—while his mother taught him the piano. Later he became the lead French horn player in the Middlesex Youth Orchestra. Then he became passionately interested in Dixieland jazz. On Sunday nights Pete and John would go to the Chiswick Jazz Club in west London. When John started the Confederates, he asked Pete to join. They played their first gig on a Saturday night at the Congregational Church Hall on Churchfield Road in Acton. Townshend said that it was the only time he was nervous on stage.

Soon after, Entwistle was lured away to another trad. jazz band. Then, after a fist-fight with the drummer, Pete left too.

The 14-year-old then acquired a very cheap Czechoslovakian-made acoustic guitar from his mother's bric-a-brac store as, with Cliff Richard and the Shadows, England was beginning to make rock and roll its own. Now the pubescent Townshend had a real incentive to learn to play the guitar. Acutely aware of his inordinately large nose and gawky looks, he felt that the only way he could get a girl was to be a rock-and-roll star.

By this time, Entwistle, who had given up the trumpet, after a brief flirtation with the guitar got into the electric bass, building one of his own. Pete and John joined up again and played with a local band called the Aristocrats. With another local band called the Scorpions, they played a gig at the nearby Congo Club. There, for the first time, Townshend realized the power of rock and roll. There were not many bands playing the new music. Townshend could feel the excitement. Even the ill-rehearsed Shadows numbers they played generated an aura of sex and violence. The gig gave him a new confidence and the guitar became his obsession.

Around that time, Roger Daltrey was playing with a band called the Detours. A working-class boy, he had been born on March 1, 1944 in Hammersmith, west London, during an air raid. Daltrey was a bright lad. He passed the 11-plus exam, which allowed him to get into Acton County Grammar School—at that time England had a selective education system—but his cockney accent and working-class attitude made him stand out among the other, middle-class, pupils. Isolated, he was disruptive.

He became a Teddy boy—a gang of early rock-and-rollers who dressed in the affected attire of Mississippi riverboat gamblers—and he turned to music for self-expression. Making his own guitar out of plywood, he formed a skiffle group, which played the do-it-yourself music that was doing the rounds at the time. Later his father gave him a store-bought electric guitar in the hope that it would encourage him in his studies. It did no good. At age 15, the troublesome Daltrey was expelled from school, ostensibly for smoking in the lavatories. He became an electrician's mate on a building site, then a sheet-metal worker in a factory. It quickly became apparent to him that the only way out of this life of soul-less toil was the new rock-and-roll music that was sweeping the U.K. So at night he played local gigs as lead guitarist of the Detours.

One day in 1960, Daltrey bumped into Entwistle, who was carrying his home-made bass back from a rehearsal, and invited him to sit in on a rehearsal with the Detours. He then invited Entwistle to join the band. After six months, they sacked their rhythm-guitar player, who only knew three chords, and invited Townshend to join because he had a new amp.

The Detours acquired a manager and got some regular bookings, although they were still playing trad. jazz along with top-20 covers. Around this time, electrified Chicago rhythm and blues was sweeping London. The leading exponents, Alexis Korner's Blues Incorporated, were playing at the nearby Ealing Club. Mick Jagger and Charlie Watts were members. Townshend saw them jamming with Keith Richards one night and was impressed by their bohemian style. What Townshend had witnessed was the birth of the Rolling Stones.

By this time, Townshend had left school and had enrolled in a four-year graphic design course at Ealing Art School.

John Lennon, Ray Davis, Keith Richards, Eric Clapton, Ron Wood, Phil May, David Bowie, and many of the later British bands came out of art school. At college Pete found himself surrounded by pretty girls for the first time and, it was there, that the painfully introverted Townshend became an ostentatious extrovert.

At art college, Townshend met Tom Wright, an American photography student from Alabama. He shared a flat in Sunnyside Road, Ealing, with Campbell "Cam" McLester from Oklahoma, and the two Americans introduced Townshend to their huge collection of American jazz, blues, soul, and R&B records. This was a revelation to Townshend, who did not even own a record player. They also introduced him to the delights of marijuana, which was rare in England back then. Townshend became a fixture in their flat, listening intently to Bo Diddley, John Lee Hooker, Leadbelly, Howlin' Wolf, Muddy Waters, Ray Charles, Jimmy Reed, James Brown, Snooks Eaglin, Jimmy Smith, Lightin's Hopkins, Slim Harpo, Buddy Guy, Sonny Terry & Brownie McGhee, Big Bill Broonzy, Little Richard, Joe Turner, Nina Simone, Fats Domino, Jerry Lee Lewis, the Isley Brothers, Carl Perkins, the Coasters, the Drifters, Bobby Bland, Jimmy McGriff, John Patton, Brother Jack McDuff, the Miracles, the Impressions, and the Shirelles.

Jazz was still a passion, and Townshend listened to John Coltrane, Charlie Parker, Miles Davis, Charles Mingus, Wes Montgomery, Mose Allison, Jimmy Guiffe, and Dave Brubeck. But from his extensive listening in this period Townshend picked out two particular influences: Steve Cropper's economic and soulful guitar work on Booker T.

& the MG's "Green Onions"—Townshend's all-time favorite track—and the inventive lyrics of Chuck Berry. It was from these raw materials that *Tommy* was forged.

Soon there were influences closer to home. In 1962, the airwaves were full of a new band from Liverpool called the Beatles. At art school, Townshend attended a lecture by the artist Gustav Metzger on the German auto-destructive art movement. Exponents produced sculptures that collapsed and pictures painted using acid so they would eat themselves away.

At college and later at Wright and McLester's flat, Townshend met the telephone engineer and jazz pianist Andrew "Thunderclap" Newman, who was experimenting with multitracking. Soon Townshend was making taped sound collages of his own.

By 1963 the Detours were opening for the big names of the time—Shane Fenton and the Fentones, Cliff Bennett and the Rebel Rousers, and Screaming Lord Sutch. Johnny Kidd and the Pirates were particularly influential as they had the four-man line-up—vocalist, drummer, bassist, and a single guitarist—that The Who would adopt. The Pirates' guitarist, Mick Green, impressed Townshend with his string-bending style borrowed from James Burton's playing on Ricky Nelson's records, and the way he combined rhythm guitar and lead parts, making up for the absence of a second guitar.

On December 15, 1963, the Detours opened for the Rolling Stones at St. Mary's Ballroom in Putney, southwest London. The Stones were promoting their second single, the Lennon and McCartney song "I Wanna Be Your Man." In Detour's eyes, Jagger was already a star and for Townshend the evening was an epiphany.

"I think we learned more about rock theater that night than any other," said Townshend.

The band watched from the wings and, just before the curtain was about to open, Townshend saw Keith Richards warming up by stretching his playing arm up and revolving it like a windmill. Townshend would purloin this as his trademark. In the business, it earned him the sobriquet "Birdman."

Daltrey's fingers were often cut and damaged from sheet-metal work, so he sold his electric guitar to Pete and dedicated himself to singing. At this point Townshend admitted that he still "couldn't play properly" and began to build up a style based on chords, while Entwistle, who now had a proper bass, helped to carry the melody. Under the influence of Lennon and McCartney and, later, Bob Dylan and Nina Simone, Townshend began writing songs, two of which were recorded at the home studio of a friend of a friend.

The first song Townshend published was called "It Was You." Released by a Beatles-clone called the Naturals in 1963, the record was a flop, and Townshend can't even remember whether his song was the A- or B-side. He still did not think of himself as a song writer. That was something that would happen to him almost by accident. He wanted to be a rock star, a guitar hero. Dressed up like one of the Shadows, in a dark suit, he would stand in front of the mirror with a guitar strung around his neck and his legs apart. However, having his song published and recorded gave him much-needed cachet at art school. He came back from the publishers full of talk of "advances" and "big money." Everyone was impressed.

In December 1963, Wright and McLester were busted for marijuana and recommended for deportation back to the U.S.

Townshend and his art-college friend Richard Barnes took over their flat in Sunnyside Road and their record collection, to which Townshend promptly introduced Daltrey. The band dropped the Beatles covers they had been doing and began playing rhythm and blues. This lost them all their fans. But then, after six months, they found that were attracting an audience three times the size of the one they had had before.

On February 1, 1964, another band called the Detours appeared on TV, so they had to change their name. The following Friday, after a gig at the Goldhawk pub in Shepherd's Bush, they went back to the Sunnyside Road flat for a brainstorming session. It was Richard Barnes who, after a joint or two, came up with the name The Who. Daltrey, who considered himself the leader of the band, gave his final approval to the name change the following day.

The switch to rhythm and blues had lost the band their drummer, who was no fan, and they made do with a number of fill-ins. One night they were playing in Greenford, west London, with a session drummer, when a guy walked up to them and said, "My mate can play better than your drummer."

So Daltrey, Entwistle and Townshend said, "Well, let's hear him then. Bring him up."

A small guy wearing a brown suit with his hair dyed ginger appeared. They played "Road Runner." At the end of it, he had broken the bass pedal and dislocated the hi-hat, and The Who thought, "This is the fella."

It was, of course, Keith Moon.

Born August 23, 1947 in northwest London, Moon was a hyperactive child and failed to impress at school. At 12, he joined the Sea Cadets—a youth organization linked to the

British Royal Navy—where he learned to play the bugle and the trumpet, before being let loose on a bass drum. When he was 16, his father bought him a drum set, which he practiced on endlessly, much to the annoyance of their neighbors.

He sat in with a number of local bands and was with Mark Twain and the Strangers when they were offered six months' work touring U.S. Army bases in Germany. But Moon, being a good deal younger then the rest, was too young to go. When he turned up at the gig in Greenford, he was a trainee electrician and, like Daltrey, he had decided that there had to be more to life.

"When we found Keith, it was a complete turning point," said Townshend. "He was so assertive and confident. Before then, we had just been fooling around."

The Who were now under the management of Helmut Gorden, a local doorknob manufacturer who fancied himself as west London's answer to Brian Epstein, the Beatles' Svengali. He employed 19-year-old publicist Peter Meaden, who had worked with Andrew Loog Oldham on publicity for the Rolling Stones. It was 1964, and he had noted the rise of the Mods, a sharp, fashion-conscious subculture that had blossomed from being a cult in central London to a citywide youth movement.

It favored stylish Italian motor scooters over the motorbikes of the leather-clad American-influenced Rockers and fights erupted between them at seaside resorts on bank-holiday weekends. Mods wore parkas, Madras cotton jackets, Fred Perry shirts, tight well-cut trousers, and bowling shoes. They even had their own drug of choice—the purple heart, an amphetamine that helped them to party all weekend. But they did not have their own music, so they borrowed American soul and Tamla-Motown, and West Indian ska and blue beat. Meaden realized that if he turned The Who into a Mod band they would have a ready-made following.

Townshend and Daltrey were quickly sold. Entwistle took a little longer to talk round. Meaden persuaded them to change their name again to the High Numbers—a "number" was Mod-speak for someone who got high on amphetamines. They began covering obscure Tamla-Motown tracks and even released a single. It was "I'm The Face"—a leading Mod was known as a Face—with "Zoot Suit" on the B-side. Both were credited to Meaden, although "I'm The Face" is a reworking of Slim Harpo's blues standard "Got Love If You Want It." By this time Daltrey and Moon had quit their jobs and the band members were being paid £20 ($30) a week.

"I'm The Face" peaked at number 49 in the U.K., but it did earn them a following among the Mods. In July 1964, 26-year-old Christopher "Kit" Lambert saw a bunch of scooters outside the Railway Hotel in Harrow—an affluent area in northwest London. Working as an assistant film director, he was planning a documentary on the latest youth phenomenon and went in to see what was going on. Inside a hot and dark back room, he found an audience of Mods hypnotized by a bunch of wild men performing on stage made out of beer crates. He was particularly impressed with Pete Townshend who was filling the room with screeching feedback from the amplifier.

He called his partner Chris Stamp, who was another ambitious assistant director. Unlike Lambert, Stamp was not a posh "public-school" boy, rather a working-class lad from east London, although his brother, the actor Terence Stamp, was already making a name for himself in the movies.

Stamp caught the band later at Watford Trade Hall, in Hertfordshire, north of London, and said, "I was knocked out. But the excitement I felt was not coming from the group. I couldn't get near enough. It was coming from the people blocking my way."

Lambert and Stamp signed the band for their documentary—then took over their management. They were not happy with the name of the band. To outsiders, the High Numbers did not imply drugs, but a chart position. It sounded too commercial and they weren't that sort of band. So by November 1964, they had reverted to the name The Who.

In London at the time, there was a battle going on between groups to see who was the loudest. As their puny amplifiers were borrowed from old radiograms, The Who hit on the idea of having huge speaker cabinets. Even if there was only a small 12-inch speaker inside, at least they looked impressive. The speaker manufacturer, Jim Marshall, then came up with the idea of fitting four 12-inch speakers instead of one, which doubled the volume. This had the added advantage, Townshend discovered, that, when he got the pick-up of his 12-stringed Rickenbacker directly in line with the speakers they would let out a howl of feedback on certain harmonics.

As both Townshend and Entwistle needed speakers they would stack them on top of each other. Marshall complained that their speakers were being maltreated. A technician pointed out that, at the volume they were playing, the speakers would shift due to the vibration and the whole lot would come crashing down.

"So what?" sneered Townshend as he knocked over the speaker stack.

He was already into maltreating the equipment.

"I tried to make guitar-playing look lethal," Townshend told *Rolling Stone* later. Realizing that he was not in the guitar-playing league of Jeff Beck or Eric Clapton, he made a point of showmanship. There was another reason for this. Most pop artists, he noted, had nice faces. With his huge nose, he did not. By leaping about the stage and abusing his instrument as violently as possible, he aimed to draw the audience's attention away from his face to his body.

He would finger a chord, then smash his guitar into the speaker, producing a deafening crash, but with a melodic reverberation. He also liked to put his guitar high above his head and spin it. One night he was doing this in the Railway Hotel, Harrow, which had a low ceiling. The Rickenbacker's neck had already been weakened by being smashed into the amplifier. As he raised the guitar, it hit the ceiling and the neck snapped off. In sheer frustration, he smashed it to bits with a mike stand. Fortunately he had another Rickenbacker with him. He got it and continued playing, as if smashing up the first guitar was all part of the act.

Word of this extraordinary event got around. The following week a huge crowd turned out to see him do it again. Townshend did not oblige. Instead, Moon kicked his drum set to pieces. Daltrey soon got in on the act by smashing up microphones.

Lambert was appalled at the expense. But for Townshend, who had been schooled in auto-destructivism, it was high art. Smashing their equipment to pieces became a fixture in the act. Lambert soon realized that the audience loved this orgy of destruction and these violent antics generated a huge amount of publicity. They smashed up some £6,500-worth (nearly $10,000) of equipment over the next three months. Not only did their destructive behavior become the core of the act, it was part of the sound. Later, Townshend would use numerous percussive guitar effects in *Tommy*, which would also be powered by Moon's maniac assault on his drums.

The Who got a try-out at the Marquee Club in London's West End on Tuesdays, traditionally the club's quiet night. The first night they played, it rained and there were only 30 in the audience. But the band then marshaled their hardcore fans from the Goldhawk. The "Hundred Faces" got free tickets. Others got in half price. After three weeks, they broke the house attendance record.

Now they needed a record deal. E.M.I. turned them down as the band were still performing covers, but then a producer from L.A. called Shel Talmy, who had worked with the Kinks, saw them. He felt he would have a winner if he could put the raw energy of their stage action onto vinyl. Did they have anything original? Townshend did.

He had recorded a 90-second demo in the Marquee's studio. It was a little more than a collection of chords stuck together. Townshend had tried to make it sound something like the Kinks to impress Talmy. It was called "I Can't Explain" and Talmy immediately recognized that it was something new and exciting. It was to be the making of the band that made *Tommy*.

who is **Tommy?**

The individual members of The Who played a key role in the making of *Tommy*. John Entwistle contributed a couple of songs and the personalities of Roger Daltrey and Keith Moon come across so forcefully that landed themselves parts in the movie version. And, as film men, their managers Kit Lambert and Chris Stamp forced the band to adopt a self-consciously visual and narrative style that would prove vital. It was also Lambert and Stamp who made the disastrous deal that eventually forced The Who to make *Tommy* to save themselves from bankruptcy.

Shel Talmy signed a one-off deal for "I Can't Explain" for The Who with Decca in the U.S. towards the end of 1964, with the record being distributed back in the U.K. on the Brunswick label. Thinking that Talmy had signed with Decca U.K.—a separate company—Lambert and Stamp signed a one-year production contract with Talmy's company Orbit Music with a four-year option. That was considered the maximum life of any band back in the 1960s.

When The Who turned up at Pye Studios, they found session musician Jimmy Page, later of Led Zeppelin, waiting to play the lead.

"But it was so simple, even I could play it," said Townshend.

Page got to play on the B-side, "Bald-Headed Woman."

Daltrey was dubious about the enterprise. He was now used to grunting and growling his way through R&B

standards. This was a pop song. But the switch did not faze Townshend at all. In fact, it was a creative watershed.

"When British kids in bands discovered R&B," he said, "what they discovered was a new way to write pop songs which was purely British."

That philosophy would take him all the way from "I Can't Explain" to *Tommy*, and beyond.

Through connections in the movie and T.V. industries Lambert managed to get The Who onto the influential Friday night pop show *Ready, Steady, Go!* and packed the audience with Who fans, while Stamp organized airplay on the pirate radio stations. "I Can't Explain" shot up the charts, reaching number eight in the U.K. on April 10, 1964. The single grossed around £30,000 ($50,000), but most of that went to the industry and the tax man. The band members got around £250 ($400) each, but with the amount of equipment they were trashing at gigs they were not even breaking even.

By the end of the year they were around £650,000 ($100,000) in debt. Stamp took a job back in the movie business to subsidize them. Meanwhile, Lambert encouraged their bad-boy image, getting them to tell outrageous lies to a gullible press about their cars and clothes, as if they had money to burn.

Townshend needed little encouragement to be controversial. He talked about The Who's "fire and aggression," boasting that they were a band with "hate built in." When the press turned up to their gigs, they cranked up the volume in an attempt to deafen them and put on a particularly spectacular orgy of destruction.

"We smash our instruments, tear our clothes and wreck everything," bragged Townshend in interviews. "The expense doesn't worry us because that would get between us and our music. If I stood on stage worrying about the price of a guitar, then I'm not really playing music. I'm getting involved with material values."

The sound track to the on-stage demolition derby was R&B, soul, and Tamla-Motown. They rarely played "I Can't Explain" on the grounds that it was "commercial." It was just the sort of bland pop song that they were trying to get away from, Townshend perversely told interviewers.

He soon came up with a more aptly aggressive anthem for the band—the brash, arrogant "Anyway, Anyhow, Anywhere," which he described as "two-and-a-half minutes of orderly disorder." He borrowed the theme from free jazz and flicked the toggle switch on his guitar to produce a sound like gun fire and Morse code. Daltrey, always a ready man with his fists, toughed up the lyrics—making the song their sole credited collaboration. And the recording howled with feedback.

Lambert spotted that pop art of Roy Lichtenstein and Andy Warhol in the U.S. and Peter Blake and David Hockney in the U.K. was all the rage and claimed that "Anyway, Anyhow, Anywhere" was "pop-art music" when it was release on May 21, 1965. This was an idea that ex art student Townshend quickly embraced.

"We stand for pop-art clothes, pop-art music and pop-art behavior," he said.

In fact, the raw feel of "Anyway, Anyhow, Anywhere," which captured the violent anarchy of their stage performance, was anything but pop art—which prided itself on being slick, commercial and highly finished. If anything it is proto-punk. But *Tommy*, with its pinballs and references to popular culture, would become an audio expression of pop art.

Pop art quickly defined the style of the band. Moon wore T-shirt with a Lichtenstein "POW!" emblazoned across the front or a colored bull's-eye borrowed from Jasper Johns. Entwistle opted for a chevron motif from op-artist Bridget Riley. Daltrey made his own op-art patterns on his pullovers with black electrical tape, while Townshend covered himself with badges, medals and military insignia gleaned from his mother's antique shop. The wearing of Victorian military memorabilia became fashionable the following year, so again The Who were ahead of the trends.

Jasper Johns later had made the American flag an icon of pop art, but Townshend had already co-opted the British flag. With its bright primary colors and its intricate geometric form, the Union Flag—or Union Jack—could have been borrowed directly from pop art's little sister, op art. Townshend hung the British flag over the speaker cabinets that he speared with his guitar at the end of the set and eventually he got a Savile Row tailor to run him up a jacket made out of the British flag. He subverted the patriotic symbol the previous generation went to war under, and gave it as an emblem to a new generation.

"Anyway, Anyhow, Anywhere" earned The Who another electrifying appearance on *Ready, Steady, Go!* The single was released in the U.K. with the *Ready, Steady, Go!* Theme tune "Daddy Rolling Stone" on the B-side and the first 1,000 copies were issued with a pop-art picture sleeve. It climbed to number ten in the U.K. chart and led to a nationwide tour. The Mod phenomenon had now spread across the whole country.

To keep up with a work rate that had them shuttling up and down the country, they turned to amphetamines. On stage they were always drunk. Keith Moon sometimes crashed out before a gig and had to be roused for a couple of hours of manic drumming before going back on the bottle again.

The band moved out of Ealing and into the posh district of Belgravia, close to Chelsea's Kings Road, which was one of the epicenters of what New York columnist John Crosby dubbed "Swinging London." Townshend lived in an apartment above Tracks' office, which Lambert filled with recording equipment to encourage Townshend's songwriting, and he urged him to write something "Wagnerian."

Lambert, with his Oxford education, introduced Townshend to the good things in life and managed to demystify classical music for Townshend.

"He said all great art is crap, and I've found that out," Townshend recalled. "We read that Mozart was doing commissions on numbered motifs and selling his copyrights. 'Oh, the bloody Prince of Denmark wants another piece of music and I'm busy. Give him 15 of number 22, six of number four, none of 58...' It was very like computer music. And, of course, Bach was a mathematician. These people have all been elevated to some kind of artistic gods."

Meanwhile Townshend befriended Brian Jones, the most experimental member of the Rolling Stones, who later died shortly after leaving the group in 1969. But Bob Dylan was the inspiration behind the band's next hit "My Generation."

It began as a folk song. Townshend did not get on well with his snooty neighbors in Belgravia and was outraged when the Packard hearse he had bought was towed away by the police after a complaint by the Queen Mother. So he wrote a simple protest song saying that the generation who had defeated Hitler did not understand the new post-war generation who had had nothing to do with the war. The band did not even want to record it. But Stamp and Lambert got Townshend to work on it. There were six or seven versions of the song before he came up with one the band approved of.

Entwistle was given a bass solo and developed a new guitar sound for the song. It was Lambert's idea to add the stammer to the vocals. This was instantly recognizable to Mods as the stammer you got from popping too many purple hearts.

When "My Generation" was released in November 1965, the B.B.C. promptly banned it on the grounds that it would offend stammerers. In fact, they were clearly terrified that the line "Why don't you all f-f-f-fade away" sounded as if the band were about to use another f-word. The single climbed to number two in the U.K., selling 300,000 copies, and it became an anthem of disaffected youth. In the U.S., it peaked at 74.

The song is now principally remembered for the line, "I hope I die before I get old." However, it was a dramatic number that went through three key changes, an idea stolen from the Kinks. It also had a boldness and clarity that would be heard again in "Pinball Wizard."

Although it was Daltrey who affected the amphetamine stutter on the record, he had stopped taking purple hearts.

"Once I got off the pill thing, I realized how much the band deteriorated through playing on speed," said Daltrey. "Musically, it really took a downturn."

On a tour of Scandinavia, Daltrey, who still felt he was leader of the band, became incensed and told the band they were a bunch of "junkies." To demonstrate his point flushed Keith Moon's pills down a toilet. The diminutive drummer attacked the former sheet-metal worker with a tambourine. Daltrey flattened Moon with a single punch.

The other three voted unanimously to throw Daltrey out the band. But the singer had recently left his wife and was living in the back of the band's van. A couple of days later, he swallowed his pride and begged to be allowed back, promising that there would be no more violent outbursts or assaults. Daltrey recalled, "I thought if I lost the band I was dead. If I didn't stick with The Who, I would be a sheet-metal worker for the rest of my life."

The others were reluctant to take him back. But they had a hit on their hands and Lambert and Stamp worked hard to persuade them to readmit their front man.

This was a crucial episode in the evolution of the band that made *Tommy*. For some time, Daltrey had been concerned about the musical direction the band was taking. He wanted to stick with what he knew and loved—rhythm and blues. The Who, he felt, had been hijacked by a pretentious middle-class college boy—Townshend—and his Ivy-League pal—Lambert—who was unashamedly gay.

For several years after the break-up and reconciliation, Daltrey could not depend on his place in the band. He was certainly no longer its leader and the musical direction was now totally in the hands of Townshend and Lambert. Moon was into the Beach Boys and the sound of Californian surf, while Entwistle—known as the Ox for his motionless stance on stage and his total dependability—would go along with whatever the others wanted.

With Lambert's encouragement, Townshend had been in a writing frenzy. The band now had enough material to put out an album. *My Generation* had eight original songs on it, plus a couple of James Brown covers. Although *My Generation* went to number five in the U.K. album charts, the band hated Shel Talmy's slapdash production. Daltrey said it was "scrappily done." Townshend called it "rubbish… it's crap."

The band wanted to break with Talmy and Lambert wanted to get out of the contract he had landed with Decca in the U.S. They had not had a single chart entry in the States, even though the Beatles had first arrived in the U.S. two years before and America was now in the midst of a full-scale British invasion.

Feeling that there was a hole in Talmy's contract, Lambert and Stamp took The Who to Robert Stigwood's Reaction label at Polydor and made a deal with Atlantic subsidiary Atco in the U.S. Townshend took over production work in the studio, giving him total artistic control over their next single "Substitute" and giving him one more string to his bow when it came to making *Tommy*. "Substitute" reached number five in the U.K. in April 1966, but again failed to make an impression on the *Billboard* Hot 100 in the U.S.

Talmy began an action in the High Court preventing them recording. So they had no alternative to go back on the road. Now they were commanding £350 ($500) a night and, with a string of hit singles behind them, were reaching an audience that extended far beyond the Mods. Artistically and stylistically they were moving on.

But tensions within the band were growing. With the Talmy suit hanging over them and a huge tax bill accruing, Townshend felt that the whole thing was going to come tumbling down any minute. Daltrey even quit, briefly. Moon, Entwistle, and Townshend soldiered on, although Moon made overtures to the Animals, who were then without a drummer, and Entwistle sought to replace bassist Clint Warwick in the Moody Blues.

"I saw myself writing film scores," recalled Townshend later, "while Keith and John saw themselves forming a group called Led Zeppelin."

Indeed, they had both threatened to walk out when Townshend hit Moon with his guitar. When things were going badly again in 1968, Entwistle and Moon discussed forming "a supergroup [that] would go down like a lead zeppelin"—a slang variation on "lead balloon." It was from this conversation in the Salvation Club in New York on April 5, 1968, that Led Zeppelin were born, albeit without Entwistle and Moon.

The only way to salvage the situation was to get the band back in the studio again. Lambert and Stamp went to Talmy's lawyers and made an out-of-court settlement that released The Who from their production contract in exchange for five per cent of all their earnings from records for the next five years. The Who then signed with Polydor in the U.K. for a £50,000 ($75,000) advance and returned to Decca in the U.S.

In late August they released "I'm A Boy," their first single for six months. Such a long gap between singles was usually the kiss of death in the U.K. in the 1960s, because things were moving so fast. This was the first indication that

Townshend had something more ambitious than a three-minute single in his head. It came from a musical he had been planning tentatively entitled *Quads*. It was set in the year 2000—which seemed far in the future in science-fiction-obsessed 1960s—at a time when you could select the gender of your children. A woman is delivered a baby of the wrong sex, so pretends her son is a girl.

Townshend had borrowed the chord structure of Henry Purcell's "Fantasia Upon One Note"—which Lambert had played him for inspiration—for the bridge. It was a device he had also used in "The Kids Are Alright," on *My Generation*. The Who's final Mod anthem, "The Kids Are Alright," was released by Brunswick the same month Reaction released "I'm A Boy". "I'm A Boy" reached number two in the U.K.; Shel Talmy's "The Kids Are Alright" number 41. Neither did anything in the U.S.

The year 1966 was a great one for classic albums. The Beach Boys released *Pet Sounds*, the Beatles *Revolver*, the Rolling Stones *Aftermath*, the Kinks *Face to Face*, and the Byrds *Fifth Dimension*. The Who had to follow suit, but they been kept out of the recording studio for most of the year. Chris Stamp made a quick deal with a music publisher that gave the members of the band £500 ($750) if they wrote two songs each. Consequently Daltrey, Entwistle, and Moon are all credited on *A Quick One/Happy Jack*, alongside Townshend. Even with these contributions, the album still had ten minutes to fill. Lambert urged Townshend to write a longer piece to fill out the second side. Townshend felt he was not up to it. Instead he took six fragments of songs he had been working on—"Her Man's Been Gone," "Crying Town," "We

Have a Remedy," "Ivor the Engine Driver," "Soon Be Home," and "You Are Forgiven"—and linked them together into a single extended work called "A Quick One While He's Away." Here, at last, was the "mini-opera" that he had sought to realize in *Quads*. As in *Tommy*, it told of a woman being unfaithful while her husband was away. Here, like his mother, she is ultimately forgiven.

The Who had kept up with the other bands and Townshend was now ready to face a bigger artistic challenge. But first they had to survive. And to do that they had to go to the U.S.

They arrived in the so-called "Summer of Love"—1967. It was then that the hippie movement that had been developing in San Francisco suddenly spread across America. If anything there was less love about than usual that year. The call for "Black Power" had just been made. The Vietnam War was in full swing. U.S. Air Force B-52s were dropping 800 tons of bombs a day on North Vietnam. China was in the grip of the Red Guards and the people of the breakaway state of Biafra in eastern Nigeria were starving to death or being massacred. But San Francisco's hippies seemed to offer an alternative to this misery. That year, the Flowerpot Men sang "Let's Go to San Francisco." Scott McKenzie added that if you went to "San Francisco (Be Sure to Wear Some Flowers in Your Hair)." He sold 5,000,000 copies of that record in the U.S. alone that summer.

The year began with the "Human Be-In" on the Polo Grounds of Golden Gate Park in San Francisco on January 14. This was to be a peaceful "gathering of the clans." Organizers visited the radicals on the Berkeley campus of the

University of California and invited them to participate on the condition that there was "absolutely no rabble-rousing." Their press release said, "Berkeley political activists and the love generation of Haight-Ashbury will join together with members of the new nation who will be coming from every state in the nation, every tribe of the young... to pow-wow, celebrate, and prophesy the epoch of liberation, love, peace, compassion, and the unity of mankind." Along with Haight-Ashbury's new bands including the Grateful Dead and Jefferson Airplane, old Beat Poets, including Allen Ginsberg, and L.S.D. guru Timothy Leary attended. In all, around 20,000 people turned out, many of them sampling the new "White Lightning" acid that was being distributed.

"The huge crowd was peaceful," said *Time* magazine, "an amazing tribute to Haight-Ashbury."

The Who were about to be shoved into the middle of this madness. They were booked to play the Monterey Festival. It was held on June 16–18, 1967 and was directly inspired by the Be-In in Golden Gate Park. But 400 miles to the south it was influenced more by the naked commercialism of Hollywood and Los Angeles than San Francisco's hippie ideology. It was designed to make money. Many of the San Francisco bands did not like Monterey's commercialism. Right up to the opening day of the Festival the Grateful Dead threatened to hold an alternative festival, but were eventually persuaded to join in. Big Brother and the Holding Company with Janis Joplin, Jefferson Airplane, Moby Grape, the Quicksilver Messenger Service, and Country Joe and the Fish, a Berkeley band that had played at the Be-In, were also there, along with such non-Bay Area acts as the Doors, the

Byrds, the Mothers of Invention, Smokey Robinson and the Miracles, Simon and Garfunkel, and Otis Redding. Scott McKenzie and The Who also appeared, along with Jimi Hendrix, who had just returned from England. Many of the bands were signed by record companies and the festival set Janis Joplin and Jimi Hendrix on the road to stardom. However, the hippie ideology was preserved by several of the San Francisco bands, who also played at an "alternative" free concert at Monterey Peninsular College nearby.

Brian Jones of the Rolling Stones was guest M.C., and Bob Dylan, Mick Jagger, Paul McCartney, and Donovan were on the Board of Directors. Bells, beads, headbands, flowers, and other hippie regalia were there in abundance. Like the Be-In, the festival was peaceful, but politicians and the media picked up on the free use of marijuana and L.S.D.

The Beatles had released their first psychedelic album *Sgt. Pepper's Lonely Hearts Club Band* on June 1, 1967. It became the soundtrack for the summer of love and the song "All You Need Is Love" particularly caught the ethos. Other artists' drug-influenced songs—including "Eight Miles High," "A Groovy Kind of Love," and "Good Vibrations"—added to the summer's mellow atmosphere.

The Golden Gate Park Be-In and the Monterey Festival served as an inspiration for similar smaller events across America that summer and *Sgt. Pepper* spawned numerous imitators. At Monterey, the record companies discovered that it was worth signing bands with long hair, funny names, and no following. This gave the impression that anything was possible, if you were a hippie. The festival also catapulted the hippie look across the globe—and some of its ideology followed. "Haight is Love" and "Make Love Not War" became universal slogans.

The Who were completely out of their depth in the middle of this. Nevertheless they donned the appropriate hippie gear. But that only made their act more shocking. The British bands that had been over in America so far had been pretty well behaved. Nothing had prepared the audience at the Monterey International Pop Festival for a bunch of hooligans from Shepherd's Bush who smashed their equipment to pieces. They were not mellow, laid-back, and full of love. They were full of violence and aggression. But that shock value alone made them a sensation.

They followed up with a ten-week, coast-to-coast tour supporting Herman's Hermits, fronted by fresh-faced Peter Noone. *Happy Jack* went to number 22. The Who were on their way to becoming one of the biggest touring bands in America and Keith Moon started a life-long obsession with trashing hotels. They arrived back in England $5,000 down.

Despite Moon's forthright approach, some of the madness of 1967's West Coast did rub off. Townshend began experimenting with L.S.D. He dropped a tab of acid on the flight home from California and had a bad trip. Back in England, he fell under the influence of the Indian guru Meher Baba, who was to have a profound effect on him and was the inspiration behind *Tommy*.

Unlike the talkative media-savvy Maharishi Mahesh Yogi, who the Beatles and Mick Jagger got together with that summer, Meher Baba was a frustrating guru. Born Merwan Sheheriarji Irani in Poona, India, he took a vow of silence on July 10, 1925, which he kept until his death on January 31,

1969. Fortunately he wrote a lot of books.

He lectured to his followers using a handheld alphabet board and hand gestures. It was his early disciples who renamed him Meher Baba, which means "compassionate father." They considered him the reincarnation of Jesus Christ, Buddha, Muhammad, and all other spiritual leaders. He explained that he had come "not to teach, but to awaken," and he was also known as "the Awakener." He also said that "things that are real are given and received in silence"—hence his vow of silence. However, his best known advice, "Do your best, then leave the results to me and don't worry—be happy," has since been shortened simply to, "Don't worry, be happy."

Meher Baba was actually a Zoroastrian of Persian descent. At the age of 19, while at college, he met an aged Muslim woman named Hazrat Babajan, whom he recognized as the first of five "perfect masters" he was to bump into over the next seven years. They were to help him find his spiritual identity, the "avatar of the age." Avatar is a Hindu term given to the earthly incarnation of a god. He put himself among Krishna, Rama, Buddha, Zoroaster, Jesus, and Muhammad.

"I am the same Ancient One, come again into your midst," he told his followers.

All major religions, he said, were simply revelations of the "the One Reality which is God." This meant he could accept followers from every faith. He encouraged them in their beliefs and never sought to proclaim a dogma or form a competing sect.

According to Meher Baba, the purpose of all life was to realize the oneness of God, who we cannot know consciously. The universe we touch, see, and sense was created as a whim by the unconscious god who wanted to know himself in conscious form. Consciousness evolved in seven states—inanimate matter such as metal or stone, then came vegetables, followed by worms or mollusks, then fish and sea creatures, birds, animals, and finally humans. Each soul has got to experience each of these forms of consciousness to become fully conscious. But that was not enough. The impressions gained in each separate form of consciousness then form a barrier between the soul and God. So the individual must then go on an inner spiritual path to gain knowledge of the "real self" which is God.

Meher Baba believed that it was his task to awaken the world to consciousness of the oneness of life through the simple expedient of love. To show this love he put himself at the service of the poor and poorly. He bathed lepers, cleaned the toilets of the untouchables, and fed the hungry. He also put himself at the service of "advanced souls" who flew in from the West and sought out others by traveling around the Indian subcontinent and beyond. A frequent visitor to the U.S. and Europe, he established the Meher Baba Spiritual Center in Myrtle Beach, southern California, in 1952 and the Avatar's Abode in Woombye in Queensland, Australia in 1958.

In the 1960s, Meher Baba attracted a following among young people who, like Townshend, had sought spiritual enlightenment through drugs, which was fashionable back then. He condemned them, saying, "drugs are harmful mentally, physically, and spiritually." This brought him to the attention of the news media.

By the end of 1967, Townshend was proclaiming that

Meher Baba was the Messiah. He called him the "divine presence, divine awareness, divine intelligence."

"He has completely and utterly changed my whole life," he said, "and through me, the group as a whole."

The rest of The Who thought he had lost it completely.

But it was under his influence that the ideas that would become *Tommy* formed. On the album Meher Baba is credited, with all due reverence, as "avatar." After all, Tommy, like Meher Baba, becomes the Messiah. And although Meher Baba was not deaf and blind, he was most certainly—although voluntarily—dumb.

In 1967, Townshend wrote the first track for what would become *Tommy*, "The Amazing Journey." He said later that the song, "in a sense tells the story of *Tommy* in a kind of synopsis." His aim with it was to push the rock format to the limit, "without making it pompous or pretentious and without making it sound like classical music."

But Townshend was already hard at work on another "rock opera" in his apartment in Wardour Street, in London's Soho. He had decided to do this after a conversation with Kit Lambert. Townshend told Lambert that he felt he would never be able to top "I Can See For Miles" as a pop song. He wanted to abandon rock and roll and find himself a bigger canvas where he could tackle some of the things that he saw going on around him in the later 1960s. He also wanted to do something "dangerous." They decided that he should attempt to write an opera.

Townshend's first plan was to link 25 songs in a piece intended for the psychedelic blues singer Arthur Brown, who had an operatic range and had recently signed with Lambert and Stamp's Tracks label. It was set in 1999 and followed the adventures of a man during the takeover of the world by the Red Chinese. Population control was a prominent issue at the time and the Chinese had temporarily abandoned their attempts to limit their spiraling population during the Cultural Revolution, which started in 1966.

"The hero goes through hundreds of different situations and there is music for each," said Townshend. "He goes out in a boat and gets shipwrecked, he has a bad nightmare, and so on. I have used sound effects for a lot of the situations with music over them."

He had begun recording in Talent Masters Studio in New York on their U.S. tour. The tape was left out one night by mistake and one of the cleaning staff damaged the first few bars. When Townshend heard about his, he threw a chair through the control room's sound-proof window, causing thousands of dollars worth of damage. The window and the tape were repaired.

Lambert listened to the demo tape and liked what he heard, but the storyline still ran to 20 scenes, which he thought was too long. So back in London, Townshend reworked the original tracks into a shorter opera called *Rael*, which began with a song called "That Motherland Feeling."

"This may well have a full orchestra on it as I have written a fugue into it," Townshend told *Beat Instrumental* in August 1967. "The opera would last a good 20 to 30 minutes so I don't know if we could use it on the next L.P."

Townshend also spent his time learning the piano and organ, as they were easier instruments to compose on. "That Motherland Feeling" featured organ and acoustic guitar.

Many of the other songs were keyboard-based.

Just when Townshend felt he was getting somewhere, Lambert accused him of pretending to be Wagner and reminded him that their next album, *The Who Sell Out*, needed another single.

"What did I have?" Townshend asked himself. "I had 'Rael.' So 'Rael' was edited down to four minutes—too long for a single in those days, ironically—and recorded in New York for that purpose. It later appeared on the album. No one will ever know what it means, it has been squeezed up too tightly to make sense."

"That Motherland Feeling" was dropped altogether. But the instrumental bridge became one of Townshend's favorite works and re-appeared in *Tommy* as "Sparks" and "Underture."

The Who Sell Out was essentially The Who's first concept album. It was built around a pastiche of jingles from the now defunct pirate stations that had first broken The Who and many of the other pop groups of the era. The idea was cooked up by Townshend and Stamp, who tried, unsuccessfully, to sell advertising space on the cover. However, like *Sgt. Pepper's Lonely Hearts Club Band*, which had come out five months earlier, the concept was not sustained throughout. But there were number of story-telling songs and the album gave Daltrey the opportunity to inhabit a number of different characters and develop the dramatic feel he would need later in *Tommy*.

On *The Who Sell Out*, the band included "I Can See For Miles," which Townshend had written the year before. It was the definitive Who track, but he had held it back in case their string of hit singles ran dry. But both album and single were a disappointment. The album reached number 13 in the U.K., with sales of just 50,000. The single stalled at ten.

"The day I saw it was about to go down without reaching any higher, I spat on the British record buyer," said Daltrey. "To me, this was the ultimate Who record, and yet it didn't sell."

There was a glimmer of hope from the U.S. "I Can See For Miles" reached number nine in the *Billboard* Hot 100, by far their best placing yet. It also got them on nationwide T.V. The album foundered at 23 in the U.S., though, one place lower than *Happy Jack*.

Then came 1968, when everything started to turn sour.

"We'd had two years of tremendous success," said Townshend, "and then something had gone wrong."

As disaster followed disaster in 1968 and the band's fortunes began to wane, Townshend was still confident that they could pull the cat out of the bag. After all, they now knew the business.

"We were masters of the art," he said. "We were the best Who-type band around."

writing Tommy

It was in 1968 that Townshend began talking in earnest about writing the rock opera that would become *Tommy*. In an interview with the *Melody Maker* journalist Chris Welch in May 1968, Townshend said that he was working on a pop opera, then entitled *Amazing Journey*. At that time, it was going to be about the spiritual journey of someone who had died in a car crash. He played Welch the tape of a song called "Now I'm A Farmer," a track that not even the rest of the band had heard yet. It was dropped from *Tommy* at an early stage but eventually appeared on The Who's 1974 album *Odds and Sods*.

Townshend said that he had been working on this opera in different forms, on and off, for a couple of years, but heavy commitments in the U.S. had held him up and he was worried that Keith West's *Teenage Opera* had given the idea of a pop opera a bad name.

Later that month, Townshend married his girlfriend, Karen Ashley, the daughter of Ted Ashley who wrote and arranged music for movies and T.V., and later conducted the London Symphony Orchestra in the 1978 version of "Pinball Wizard." They moved into a three-story Georgian townhouse in Twickenham, a wealthy suburb to the west of London. It overlooked the River Thames opposite Eel Pie Island—then home to a famous rock venue. Eventually he spent £8,000 ($12,000) installing a recording studio, which boasted a state-of-the-art eight-track tape recorder. But for *Tommy* he used two old Revox stereo tape players that had come from his Belgravia studio. Overdubbing from one machine to the other, he could produce a sound that the band could replicate. Along with the two-tape machine, he had an old but well-made microphone mixer, an electric piano, a drum set donated by Keith Moon, two organs, a set of bongos, numerous guitars, an electronic limiter, and other devices for producing sound effects such as echo and reverberation, plus a vast collection of records. On the bookshelves were the scores of the operas *La Traviata* by Giuseppe Verdi and *Faust* by Charles Gounod, along with books by Meher Baba and volumes of Persian and Sufi poetry. Meher Baba's picture also graced the walls. It was here that Townshend would write *Tommy*, but first The Who had to the tour the States again.

In San Francisco in June, Townshend was interviewed by Jann Wenner of *Rolling Stone* magazine in . In the interview, Townshend outlined the whole story of the concept album he intended to call *Deaf, Dumb and Blind Boy*. It was about a boy who was born deaf, dumb, and blind—although this was to change later—and what happened to him in his life. The boy was to be played by The Who as a musical entity and would be represented by a theme that would run throughout what Townshend was already called "the opera."

Because the boy was deaf, dumb, and blind, he experienced the world only through vibrations, which he translated into music. The listener would become aware of the boy because the band would be creating him—or at least the world around him—as they played.

In the interview Townshend mentioned things that ended up as important elements in *Tommy*—not least that name.

"He feels his mother's touch, he feels his father's touch," said Townshend, "but he just interprets them as music."

His father gets frustrated because he can't play soccer with this son like other British dads. He gets drunk one night and leans over the kid's bed and says, "Can you hear me?"

Of course, the child cannot hear him. He just smiles and in frustration his father starts to hit him. This was a part Townshend said he intended to give to Keith Moon to interpret.

Later on in the "opera," the mother and father go out, leaving the child in the hands of his uncle, who was, "a bit of a perv." He sexually molests the boy. During this he gets to hear his own name, "Tommy."

"He's really got this big thing about his name," said Townshend.

He also mentioned that there would be a doctor who tried some psychiatric treatment.

"The second important event is when he sees himself in the mirror, suddenly seeing himself for the first time," said Townshend. "To us, it's nothing to be able to see and hear and speak, but for him it's absolutely incredible and overwhelming."

The project, he said, was already well advanced.

"Lyrically, it's quite easy to do; in fact, I've written it out several times," said Townshend. "It makes great poetry."

It was the music that was going to be the problem.

"The music has to explain what happens," he said.

During the tour, Townshend discussed the project with the other band members on planes and in hotel rooms and they warmed to it.

"Roger seemed to quite like the idea," said Townshend about this early stage of the project. "Keith would always go along with whatever I suggested, and John quite liked the idea and wanted to write something for it."

This tour pulled them together. The old acrimony was gone. Zigzagging back and forth across America, they were four Englishmen in a sea of what—to them—were foreigners. The hardships of touring build band solidarity and their triumphs on stage encouraged the feeling that, if they just stuck together, they would make it.

When they got back to England, they knew that the rock opera brewing in Townshend's brain would be the making of them. Otherwise they were finished. So they left him alone to get on with it, even though they were all now desperately short of money.

By now Townshend had complete confidence in his songwriting ability. He had already proved—with "Substitute," "I'm A Boy," and "Pictures of Lily (the last was released in the U.K. only in April, 1967)—that he could write songs about absolutely anything. People said he had talent, or even genius, but to him the songwriting process was still a bit of a mystery.

"I would love to be able to say it was just 'hard work,'" said Townshend. "But often the harder I worked at something, the less real and connected with its audience—and my own life—it became."

Townshend already knew that when he wrote something surprising often happened, even in an ostensibly simple song. He realized that *Tommy* had to develop unconsciously. Indeed, it was already happening. Although he had often thought about writing a rock opera and had made several attempts before, he had not worked out the story of *Tommy* before that interview with Jann Wenner. That had happened late at night after a grueling three-hour gig at San Francisco's Fillmore West. Townshend had gone back to Wenner's house, exhausted. He complained throughout the interview that he was not at all "together." But when Wenner asked him what ideas for future work he had, his vision of the completed work just came tumbling out. *Rolling Stone* printed the interview verbatim, "and that became my blueprint... The book for *Tommy* is that *Rolling Stone* article," said Townshend.

Earlier, when they had toured the U.S. as support for Herman's Hermits, Townshend had been rushing back to the hotel after each show to write down ideas for the rock opera, scribble songs, or collate lyrics. Back in the calm of Twickenham, Townshend looked through his notes. There were numerous sheets of lyrics and number of completed songs that he had forgotten about. These became the core of *Tommy*.

It was not until much later that Townshend realized that *Tommy* was essentially autobiographical. At the time he was writing it, he thought of the project as a religious quest. He wanted the opera to tell a "a spiritual story in a parallel way, from the inside and the outside." The material he was looking through, like his other work, was very solid and concrete. However, because of his discovery of Meher Baba, he was in a very spiritual mood.

"I was captivated," said Townshend, "but felt that The Who had absolutely no hope. Keith Moon and spiritual revolution? Roger Daltrey, a sheet-metal worker from Acton, and spiritual revolution? But I could do it. Of course, I could."

Instead of writing more songs, he spent much of his time writing prayers to Meher Baba. These filled his conscious mind while *Tommy* took shape at a deeper level. But Meher Baba was not the only influence. Townshend said that he was also taken with the writing of George Adamski.

Adamski was a Polish American, who was one of the first people to claim to have been contacted by aliens and chronicled his adventures with the "space people" in several books. Born in Poland in 1891, he emigrated to the U.S. with his family, aged two. After serving with the 13th U.S. Cavalry and the National Guard, he received an honorable discharge in 1919.

In 1926, he settled at Laguna, California, where he began lecturing on oriental philosophy, although he had no formal training. In 1940, he moved to Valley Center, California, where he established a cult movement known as the Royal Order of Tibet. As its spiritual leader, Adamski became a self-styled professor of philosophy. It was there on October 9, 1946, that Adamski claimed to have seen a "dirigible-shaped mother ship" flying over his home. Adamski said that his sighting was a sign and the cult settled on the southern slopes of Mount Palomar, near the observatory. From there, he set out to make contact with the aliens he believed were visiting the planet.

On November 20, 1952, he took six friends out on a picnic in the Mojave Desert in California. A gigantic cigar-shaped craft glided silently into view. It was chased away by military jets—but ejected a silver disc, which landed some distance away. Adamski and two of his friends motored off into the desert after it, hoping to get a closer view and take some photographs of it. At the end of a dirt road, Adamski set up his portable telescope and took a number of photographs of the silvery craft. Then he ventured nearer to it to get some close-ups.

The alien craft shot skywards and soared out into space. A few minutes later, a second, smaller saucer-shaped craft appeared, gliding between two mountain peaks some way ahead of Adamski. He watched and photographed the craft as it landed about 1,200 feet away. A figure got out and beckoned to him. At first Adamski thought the figure was a man. "But the beauty of his form surpassed anything I had ever seen," Adamski recalled later. The humanoid was short, about 63 inches tall, with smooth, tanned skin and long blond hair, and was dressed in a brown one-piece suit, with a broad belt, and red shoes.

Adamski shook hands with the being, and the two began communicating telepathically. The creature's name was Orthon, Adamski said. He came from Venus, where the Venusians lived a pure, spiritual, and God-fearing way of life. He had come to Earth to warn humankind about the dangers of nuclear energy and pollution. After refusing to be photographed, Orthon stepped into his craft and shot off back into space.

This tale was recounted at great length by Adamski in his book, *Flying Saucers Have Landed*, in 1953 and was the first of many meetings with Venusians. Adamski lectured widely and his cult following grew. Those who came to hear him were told of strange journeys to distant worlds. The Venusians, he said, had come to Earth again and had taken him to Venus, the Moon, and Mars. He backed his claims with photographs of alien craft he said he had taken through his telescope. A month after his first alien contact, he photographed a

"Venusian scout craft," 35 feet in diameter, hovering above his home in Palomar Gardens, California. And in 1951, he snapped the cigar-shaped "mother ship" hovering, ready to take him on an interplanetary jaunt. He also supplied detailed drawings of the interior. Newspapers around the world lapped it up.

Flying Saucers Have Landed became an instant bestseller. Two years later his adventures reached a worldwide audience with *Inside the Flying Saucers*, in which he recounted his experiences on board the Venusians' ship and described in great detail life on the still-to-be-explored Moon. There were forests, lakes, wooded valleys, and snow-covered mountains on the lunar landscape and citizens of the Moon "strolled down the sidewalks" in lunar cities, just as humans did in Earth cities, he said. The aliens informed Adamski that the Earth was being visited by beings from the Solar System and beyond.

Adamski's third book, *Flying Saucer Farewell*, was published in 1961. By then, he was being viewed by a more educated and skeptical audience: on September 12, 1959, the Soviets had managed to hit the Moon with their probe Lunik 2 and, on October 4, 1959, Lunik 3 orbited the Moon and sent back pictures of the far side. There were no forests, lakes, wooded valleys, or snow-capped mountains to be seen. Nor were there any cities. The lunar surface was a barren stretch of rocks, dust and craters.

Adamski died on April 23, 1965, just as a series of new probes, both Soviet and American, was heading for the Moon. At best, it can be said that Adamski made wild exaggerations, which certainly destroyed any reputation he may have had.

Today, he is largely dismissed as a fraud. However, when he died he left behind a collection of photographs and film footage, many of which have still not been discredited. His photographs of "mother ships" and their "scout craft" may seem too good to be true, but while skeptics have mocked them, no one has proved them to be fakes.

Like Adamski, Townshend had an interest in Eastern religion and said that he drew inspiration for *Tommy* from the work of Nobel Prize-winning writer Herman Hesse, in particular *Siddhartha*, the novel he wrote in 1922. His works deals with the duality of spirit and nature, body versus mind, and the individual's spiritual search outside the restrictions of the society to discover their essential nature.

Hesse published his first works, *Romantische Lieder* and *Eine Stunde Hinter Mitternacht* in 1899. He became a full-time writer in 1904, when his novel *Peter Camenzind* gained literary success. In 1911 he visited India and became interested in Eastern religions. The ancient cultures of the Hindus and the Chinese had a great influence on Hesse's works.

In 1912 Hesse and his family took up permanent residence in Switzerland. Hesse spent the years of World War I there, his writing attacking the prevailing moods of militarism and nationalism. He became a permanent resident of Switzerland in 1919 and a citizen in 1923.

Crises in his personal life led Hesse into psychoanalysis under J.B. Lang, a disciple of Carl Gustav Jung. This led to his breakthrough novel, *Demian*, published in 1919. It was a Faustian tale of a man torn between his orderly bourgeois existence and a chaotic world of sensuality, and his struggle for self-awareness.

Leaving his family in 1919, Hesse moved to Montagnola, in southern Switzerland. There he set to work on *Siddhartha*, a novel of asceticism set in the time of the Buddha. When translated into English in 1954, it became a powerful influence on the American Beat Poets.

The book takes its title from Siddhartha Gautama, the name of the man who became the Buddha. It begins with a grizzled ferryman sitting listening to the river in the shade of a banyan tree. His name is also Siddhartha. Born the son of a Brahmin, Siddhartha was blessed in appearance, intelligence, and charisma. But he discarded his promising future to search for the meaning of life as a wandering ascetic. For a while he followed the Buddha but left to follow the dictates of his own soul. However, true happiness evaded him. Then a life of pleasure and titillation eroded away his spiritual gains and he became the pathetic prisoner of his own whims and desires. However, now that he was a simple ferryman, local people considered him to be a sage.

Hesse's books often describe the struggles of young men and, like other Hesse protagonists, Siddhartha has a strong strain of European angst and stubborn individualism. His final epiphany runs contrary to both Buddhist and Hindu ideals of enlightenment. He is neither a practitioner nor a devotee and does not meditate or recite religious texts. Instead he becomes one with the world of nature, finding harmony in its rhythms, and he begs the reader to seek answers from the river.

In 1927 Hesse published the novel *Der Steppenwolf*, which describes the conflict between bourgeois acceptance and the spiritual self-realization of a middle-aged man. Again, this was enormously influential when translated into English in 1963. In 1967, a West Coast psychedelic band— famous for the songs "Born to be Wild" and "The Pusher" that featured in the 1969 hippie road movie *Easy Rider*— took its name from the book's title.

During the Weimar Republic (1919-1933) Hesse stayed aloof from politics. In 1931 he began work on his masterpiece, *Das Glasperlenspiel*, which again explores the dualism of the contemplative life and real life.

Although Townshend continued to drink and smoke cigarettes, under the influence of Meher Baba, he had given up the L.S.D. that had made him almost completely unproductive the previous year. However, *Tommy* takes much of its psychedelic imagery from Townshend's experiences under the influence of acid.

After spending a great deal of time praying and examining himself and his motives, Townshend eventually got down to the business of writing *Tommy*. He began shakily. His confidence had been shaken by the failure of *Rael*. First he had to work out what had gone wrote. Townshend came to believe that *Rael* failed because it was a political story and he did not have much of a head for politics. He had also intended *Rael* to be performed on stage, accompanied by a full orchestra, like a conventional opera. This time he wanted to create a vehicle for the group, one where the characters of each individual member could shine through. Despite Kit Lambert's urgings, Townshend decided that he was not going to attempt to produce recitative operatic music or make *Tommy* function as a conventional opera. Essentially *Tommy* is a series of pop songs that tell a story, linked by shorter musical fragments that help carry the narrative forward.

"The ingredients of the songs aren't there to put across a mood, or a feeling of an age, or a feeling of society," said Townshend. "They're meant to tell a direct story in a literary manner."

Townshend's songwriting method was to produce demos. or test recordings, which he presented to the band for their approval. He did this because he knew he was very impulsive and often quite self-revealing when he wrote. If he went to the lengths of producing a demo, he could be fairly sure that nothing would be included in the final song that he might regret later. He also found that a demo gave him a fairly good idea of whether a song was good or not and whether it would be worth completing. There were occasions, though, when Townshend found that a completely new song that he had not thought about earlier emerged spontaneously in the studio.

At home, he experimented with various arrangements, adding drum, keyboard, bass, or guitar parts. Even when he made a mistake, he found the process productive because an error effectively eliminated one of the numerous possibilities that always present themselves in songwriting. The demos he produced usually had a lighter, less solemn feel to them than the finished work and relied more heavily on the use of the electric organ.

The electric organ was in vogue at the time. It had become a popular instrument in 1967 with Procol Harum's "Whiter Shade of Pale," a drug-inspired song based on Bach's cantata, "Sleepers Awake." The Crazy World of Arthur Brown, Julie

Driscoll, the Doors, Brian Auger and the Trinity, and the Nice all used the organ around that time. Even Bob Dylan got in on the act. But by the early 1970s the synthesizer had taken over and the organ began to sound dated. Fortunately on the final cut of *Tommy*, the organ was used sparingly. Although *Tommy* was very much a studio album, The Who knew that they would have to reproduce it on stage, where, with just the four of them, there would be no one else to play it. But the fact that the organ was used so little on the final version gave *Tommy* a wider and more lasting appeal.

Generally the songs on *Tommy* were structured around chord progressions on an acoustic guitar with embellishments on the electric guitar. They reproduced the format established on *The Who Sell Out*, using a guitar, bass, and drums with three-part vocal arrangements. As the story called for a number of different characters, Townshend and Entwistle were required to sing more lead vocals than on their other albums. Townshend added the occasional piano and organ parts, while Entwistle provided horn and brass. But no attempt was made to reproduce the sound of the band playing live. The stage show would have to follow the album, not the other way around.

The central figure, Tommy, had developed out of Damon, the protagonist of *Rael*. That name had been borrowed from the band's sound engineer Damon Lyon-Shaw and Townshend had used the name Damon because he thought it exotic. Tommy was much more down to earth name. Tommy, in England, is every man. It is John Doe, Joe Schmo, or—more accurately—G.I. Joe. Tommy Atkins is the tradition name for a private soldier in the British Army. World Wars I and II were very much within living memory in the 1960s and during those wars much of the male population had been mobilized. Everyone in Britain knew someone who had been a "Tommy."

Townshend said that the name Tommy had come into his mind "from mid-air." He liked the fact that it was associated with war and heroism. That made it a good name for a protagonist. But he also spotted spiritual dimensions to the name. The middle letters were "om"—the mantra chanted by Hindus when contemplating the ultimate reality. And to Townshend the name Tommy also said "to me," which obviously gave it other spiritual connotations.

In *Rael* Townshend had given Damon a lisp. This time he had gone further, making Tommy deaf, dumb, and blind. Townshend was fascinated by freaks, especially those who had triumphed despite their freakiness. This drew him to producing the portly "Thunderclap" Newman. Although Newman was the antithesis of a rock star, Townshend gave him a number-one hit single in the U.K. with "Something In The Air." It got a great deal of airplay in the U.S., but only made number 37 in the *Billboard* charts. At one time, he also planned to produce Tiny Tim, a stringy-hair, big-nosed, baggy-suited weirdo who sang 1920s show tunes in a falsetto voice, accompanying himself on the ukulele, and rather mysteriously became one of the big novelty acts in the late 1960s and early 1970s.

Townshend also thought that making Tommy deaf, dumb, and blind was the perfect allegory for the spiritual ignorance of humankind as revealed by Meher Baba. Although in our ordinary lives, our five senses are fully functioning, Meher Baba preached that there were whole chunks of life that we were not conscious of. Blinded by what we do see, feel, and hear, we miss the whole concept of reality. We do not understand life because we cannot see beyond it. We cannot accept death, although it is just part of the wheel of life. And we feel that the suffering we experience on Earth is unjust because we refuse to see what motivates it. So by making Tommy deaf, dumb, and blind, Townshend aimed to show that the glaring gaps in his perception reflected our own.

Townshend sought support from other followers of Meher Baba, including Ronnie Lane, bassist of the Small Faces. His most important mentor at that time was the painter Mike McInnerney, who had introduced him to the writing of Meher Baba in the first place. Later, McInnerney designed the cover of *Tommy* and produced seven paintings for the booklet that accompanied the double album.

He would play the demo tapes to McInnerney, ostensibly so that he would have an idea of what sort of artwork was needed for the cover. But in reality, he did it to judge his reaction. Townshend said that it was largely McInnerney's appreciation of what he was doing that kept the ideas flowing and the project moving ahead.

Having friends listen to his demos was not always a good idea. One evening he invited his friend, Richard Stanley, who was staying with Townshend and his wife at the time, up to his studio to hear the demo for the track "Welcome." To Townshend the song reflect his state of mind and the progress he was making in his spiritual journey and he wanted to share it. But when Stanley heard the lines, "Come to this house, and be one of comfortable people, Come to this house and be one of us," and thought they were an invitation for him to join Townshend and Karen in a *menage à trois*, if not group sex. There was embarrassment all around.

Nevertheless, Stanley continued to be a sounding board for Townshend to bounce ideas off. Indeed, it had been Stanley to whom Townshend had shown the two lines on a piece of paper that contained the original idea of *Amazing Journey*—and thus *Tommy*—the year before. Stanley was a particularly useful critic because he was more interested in music than the mysticism of Meher Baba.

Admittedly, Stanley had been confused by Townshend two-line concept statement. It talked of the confusion between illusion and reality. Townshend had come to believe everything we see in the world and take for reality is, in fact, an illusion. Reality, he thought, was a mystical thing that lay beyond what we can see, hear, touch, or smell. The truth was hidden and was revealed slowly and painfully through experience. It was only at the end of a long spiritual path that one came up against immutable and timeless reality. On the other hand, when Townshend re-read the two-line concept he had shown Stanley ten years later, he found it confusing too.

At the outset *Amazing Journey* was to be a series of linked songs that switched alternately between illusion and reality while charting the spiritual progress of the story's young protagonist. However, Townshend soon abandoned this idea. It was simply too unwieldy to have two songs about each event—one showing what appeared to be happening and one spelling out what really happened. Jumping back and forth this way between two points of view would leave the listener confused. Instead Townshend aimed to meld the two points of view together in a more organic fashion.

Around this time Townshend discovered that his central figure, Tommy, and his awakening were more than metaphor. Researching autism, Townshend came across the work of Professor Paul Nordoff. A graduate of the Philadelphia Conservatory of Music and the Juilliard Graduate School, Nordoff had been a professor of music, a noted composer, and a gifted pianist before he witnessed the response of disabled children to music. In 1961, he set up a day care unit for autistic children where he developed music therapy. He went on to develop other therapies for psychotic, physically disabled, and communicatively handicapped children. By 1967, his techniques had spread to Germany, Italy, Holland, and Britain, and he produced three books on the subject. Townshend noted that Nordoff had used a combination of love and music to reconnect deaf, dumb, and blind kids to the outside world. He was now convinced of the truth of his vision.

Townshend already had "Sparks" and "Underture" from *Rael*, and "Amazing Journey" and "Welcome" had also been written. And he had a song called "Sensation." It had been written as a straightforward pop song aimed at a girl Pete had met on The Who's disastrous tour of Australia in early 1968. The lyric ran "… She's a sensation…" But it was a simple matter to change that line to "He's a sensation."

Another gender-change gave Townshend another *Tommy* song. He had written "Glow Girl" while on tour in the U.S. with Herman's Hermits, when he was on a plane that he was convinced was going to crash. Although the song was considered for release as a single at the time, it did not see the light of day until it appeared on the compilation album *Odds and Sods* in 1974. In the song, a girl and her boyfriend are on a plane that catches fire. The crash is simulated with guitar feedback. Then a softer tune emerges indicating that the couple have been reincarnated as a baby. The line is, "It's a girl, Mrs. Walker, it's a girl." With a switch of sex, this is the core of "It's A Boy."

He also had most of "We're Not Gonna Take It." It was originally a song about Fascism. The final section, "Listening to you, I get the music," was added later. "See Me Feel Me" comes from the song "I Can't Reach You," on *The Who Sell Out*, which contains the line, "See, feel, or hear from ya."

These songs had all been written as separate entities, some of them even before Townshend had conceived the idea for *Tommy*. But now when he brought them together, they all fitted into the large scheme of things.

Roughly 24 years after the event, he told *Rolling Stone*, "When I sat down to write *Tommy*... my prime objective was to... say listen, the three-minute rock song is so effective that if you string a bunch of them together you can deal with a much bigger idea, a spiritual idea, perhaps the idea that we are all living a dream."

Townshend also picked up "Eyesight for the Blind," an old blues number written by Sonny Boy Williamson, who had died in 1965. This actually talks of restoring eyesight to the blind and bringing hearing to the deaf, so it proved rather useful. At this point "Now I'm A Farmer" was rejected.

"Tommy's Holiday Camp" was written much later when they were in the studio. Townshend had been worried about the ending of the opera. After Tommy had been elevated to the roll of the Messiah, some sort of "church" had to be established around him. But Townshend did not want to include anything "churchy" on the album, fearing that it would make the work too pretentious. One night when they were leaving the I.B.C. Studios where they were recording the album, he was explaining this to Keith Moon who said it would be a good idea if the whole thing was set in a holiday camp.

Although most holiday camps in Britain closed down in the 1980s, they were very much part of British life in the 1950s and 1960s. Originally started in the 1930s, they provided cheap accommodation in self-contained chalets. All meals were included in the price of the vacation, along with use of swimming pools, dance halls, theaters, and other facilities. Crèches for infants and entertainment for youngsters were also provided, so that parents could have a little time to themselves. There was a huge growth in the provision of holiday camps in the late 1940s. After the long privations of World War II and post-war rationing, the British people needed cheap vacations. Ex-servicemen, of course, were used to camp life. However, with the boom in cheap flights to the Mediterranean that began in the late 1960s, the British started to take all-inclusive vacations in Spain or the Balearics and those still staying in holiday camps were seen as unadventurous and low class.

Townshend agreed that the finale should be set in a holiday camp and Moon said that he would write a song about it that night. But Townshend was afraid that anything Moon would write might clash with the overall feel of the work. So he told Moon that he had already written the song.

"I think he took my point," said Townshend.

At home that night, Townshend wrote a short piece called "Ernie's Holiday Camp" which became "Tommy's Holiday Camp." Although Moon did not write the song, it was credited it to him because Townshend thought that it turned out exactly the way Moon would have written it.

"Pinball Wizard"—which is essentially the climax of the album—was also written late in the recording cycle. The idea of the pinball Messiah came from Nik Cohn, Britain's foremost rock critic in the 1960s. At the time he was working for the *Guardian*, before moving to *The New York Times*. He was a close friend of both Kit Lambert and Pete Townshend, and was a pinball fanatic. His girlfriend at the time was a pinball champion and he was writing a novel called *Arfur—Teenage Pinball Queen*, which was published the following year.

Townshend had played some of the demo tapes to Cohn, whose response was lukewarm about the project. Afterwards they met up in a pinball parlor, where Cohn said that a rock opera about a protagonist going on a spiritual journey was essentially pretentious and boring.

"If Tommy was a pinball player, would you be more receptive to the idea?" Townshend asked.

Cohn stopped playing for a second and said, "Yeah."

Townshend went home that evening and wrote what he considered an "awful... clumsy" song. It was "Pinball Wizard." Then he set about rewriting the whole piece around Tommy the pinball player rather than Tommy the boy on a spiritual quest—"so the pinball becomes a metaphor for the life of a rock star or even the life of a guru," said Townshend.

He then went back to Cohn and ran it by him again. This time he was impressed.

"It's great, it works," said Cohn. "It's not just great because you've done this for me and I will give it a good review, what it's actually done is it's added some color and some real pop to this otherwise really quite boring idea about... the spiritual life."

Ultimately Townshend felt that this change in the setting compromised the work.

"I suppose the mistake I made in *Tommy* was, instead of having the guts to take what Meher Baba said—which was 'Don't worry, be happy, leave the results to God'—and repeat that to people, I decided the people weren't capable of hearing that directly," he said. "They've got to have it served in this entertainment package. And I gave them *Tommy* instead, in which some of Meher Baba's wonderfully explicit truths were presented to them half-baked in a lyric form and diluted as a result."

That idea persisted. Even years after the release of *Tommy*, Townshend claimed "the definitive *Tommy* album is still in my head."

"Cousin Kevin" and "Fiddle About"—about Tommy's physical abuse at the hands of his yobbish cousin and his sexual abuse at the hands of Uncle Ernie—were written by John Entwistle, who had already demonstrated his ability with macabre lyrics with "Doctor Doctor," "Dr. Jekyll and Mr. Hyde," and "Medac." Townshend said that they were in the studio. He was busy writing other songs and simply told Entwistle to go away and "write something horrible."

The way Entwistle remembered it, Townshend had given him the writing commission earlier.

"I remember being in Detroit on the 'Magic Bus' tour"—in

July 1968—"and we had a *Tommy* meeting," Entwistle said. "Pete suggested two songs he felt he couldn't write. Basically the brief I got was to write a song about a homosexual experience with a nasty uncle and a song about being bullied by... I don't know whether a cousin was actually mentioned, but I figured that it might as well be the son of Uncle Ernie. I wrote those songs very quickly. If someone gives me a subject to write about, I get it done."

It has to be said that Entwistle's songs are creepy. But that did not matter to Townshend. He saw everything that happened to Tommy as part of his spiritual awakening.

"He gets everything in a very pure, [un]filtered, unadulterated, unfucked-up manner," said Townshend. "Like when his uncle rapes him, he is incredibly elated, not disgusted, at being homosexually raped. He takes it as a move of total affection, not feeling the reasons why. Lust is a lower form of love, like atomic attraction is a lower form of love. He gets an incredible spiritual push from it, where most people would a get a spiritual retardment, constantly thinking about this terrible thing that's happened to him. In Tommy's mind everything is incredible, meaningless beauty."

Years later, Townshend admitted to having homosexual experiences himself.

Townshend set about the structure of the opera in a more formal way. A simple list of songs and events developed into complex charts showing the parallels between reality and illusion. These show the influence of the spiritual journey that Townshend believed he was taking under the guidance of Meher Baba. But again that approach proved too cumbersome and was abandoned. Instead, he wrote out the story as a simple narrative. This, he said, read like poetry—sometimes good poetry, sometimes bad. A lot was just written down as a stream of consciousness. When he read it back he said he was "staggered." It read like a story that he could not possibly have dreamed up himself, let alone been able to express in music. He found that many of the songs that he already had, fitted. Others, though, had to be reworked as Townshend wanted to give the impression that, when Tommy walked out of one song, he walked directly into the next.

Looking back at his notes ten years after the event, Townshend was also struck by the fact that there seemed to be no intermediate stages of development from his original efforts at producing a deliberately Hermann Hesse-style plot and the final version. It was as if *Tommy* had arrived fully formed.

Townshend was conscious that the album must not directly proselytize the views of Meher Baba. The last thing a rock audience wanted was preaching. However, the moment when Tommy regained his sight, hearing, and ability to speak mirrored the spiritual awakening that Townshend felt he had experienced. And, in the final version, *Tommy* becomes the story of a kind of 20th-century Christ.

"The general theme of the album is a direct result of me getting involved with Baba, getting involved in a powerful spiritual move forward," he said. "I think it is more powerful because of that very reason, because the project has got a very high ideal to it."

With these theological underpinnings, Townshend felt that even such a hard-edged materialist band like The Who could not disguise the mystical values of the story. Even though the original intention had long been subsumed, realism took over from mysticism, and the music was commercial pop, Townshend felt that the strong thread of spirituality remained.

Normally, such sentiments would run the risk of making the resulting work pretentious. But in the case of *Tommy* this does not happen because the album was delivered by a four-piece rock group at the height of its powers.

recording Tommy

Some of the demo tapes Townshend had produced, he admitted were really rather "dreary." Nevertheless the band were committed to the project. And on September 19, 1968, The Who went into Studio A at London's I.B.C. Studios in Portland Place, next to the B.B.C.'s Broadcasting House.

The initials I.B.C. stood for International Broadcasting Company and the studios had been designed for use by commercial radio stations abroad. Until 1972, there was no commercial broadcasting in Britain because the B.B.C. maintained a monopoly. So commercial stations had been set up overseas—and later on "pirate" ships around the coast—to broadcast back to the U.K. The studio was not the most technically advanced, but Kit Lambert hired it because it was cheap. This meant that the band could spend an extended period in the studio and Lambert block-booked it for eight weeks.

The "producer-in-charge" was Kit Lambert, although Townshend himself would be responsible for the sound quality and balance. He would work closely with Damon Lyon-Shaw as he cut the tracks onto an eight-track tape. While Lambert had been influential in the whole idea of producing an opera, he wanted to stand back from the story's mystical theme and adopt a more objective view. He was more interested in producing a "rock opera" than a "god opera."

The demos were presented to the band, who then worked up their own parts. Townshend saw little point in trying to tell Keith Moon how to play the drums, John Entwistle how to produce a melodic bass track, or Roger Daltrey how to interpret a lyric. They were all masters in their own field. But Kit Lambert wanted to bring in an orchestra to give the piece a more operatic feel. The band resisted this. They figured that because they were going to have to reproduce the opera on stage, they could only use the instruments that the four of them could manage.

"If it was written for The Who, it was obviously gonna be a stage piece," said Townshend. "We were a performing band. We weren't a studio band like the Beatles had become... we can't do a *Sgt. Pepper*-type thing, we can't do a *Pet Sounds*-type thing. We can't do a studio masterpiece. We have to do something we can play. That's why *Tommy* is so simple. That's why it's so unorchestrated, so... unscrewed around with in the studio... We kept it really simple because we wanted to play it. So in a sense—although it was recorded—it was recorded and composed for the stage. It had to work live."

For the same reason, they largely banned sound effects. At one time it was proposed that there should be a sequence of battle sounds following "Overture" and that the sound of a pinball machine should be heard in the linking instrumental tracks known provisionally as the "Dream Sequence." But in the end, The Who decided that *Tommy* was to be a pure rock album. It should only include the sounds they could produce as a four-piece band.

They limited themselves to electric and acoustic guitar, organ, piano, drums, tympani, bass, trumpet, French horn, gong, tambourine, and, of course, vocals. However, Lambert did manage to persuade Townshend to begin with a formal overture, so that the finished piece would have the form of a proper opera. Lambert also encouraged Townshend's most arty flight of fancy.

"You've got to be pretentious," he would say. "You've got to go for gold. You've go to be over the top."

Townshend found Lambert's overinflated view quite amusing—and useful.

"As a kind of agitator in the music business, he was wonderful," said Townshend, "because, instead of devaluing the whole thing, he was actually making it real."

Besides, by this time, they were committed. Three days after they arrived in the studio an interview with Pete Townshend appeared in *The New York Times*, in which he talked specifically about their plans.

"I know people want something new," he said. "They want a new reason to go to a rock-and-roll concert. What we're going to try is opera, not something trashy like the pompous arty types do. They do fancy things because they can't play. We've done mini-operas, now we want a long thing around a theme. I've been thinking of a story—about a deaf, dumb, and blind kid, with dialog, action, and an incredible finale. I want to get into stuff that will leave the smashing way behind."

The album was supposed to be ready for the Christmas market, but they found that the recording took much longer than they originally thought. Despite Townshend's initial work, the band found that the concept had not been fully worked out. Townshend often had to go home at night to write new material to play to the band next day. It was a slow and painstaking process.

"Pete used to come in some days with only half a demo," said Daltrey. "We used to talk for hours, literally. We probably did as much talking as we did recording, sorting out arrangements and things."

Everything was thrashed out through debate, most often in a nearby pub.

"It was approached in exactly the way anti-intellectual rock people would hate," said Townshend. "We went into it in depth before we worked out the plot. We worked out the scatological implications, the religious implications, and the rock implications. We made sure every bit was... solid. When we'd done that we went into the studio, got smashed out of our brains and made it. Then we listened, pruned, and edited very carefully, then got smashed and did it all again."

Townshend said he was amazed at how supportive everybody in the band was—"I mean, what other three musicians would have put up with all my bullshit in order to get an album out?"

They also had to make money, so they could only work in the studio from Monday through Thursday. On the weekends, they would play shows all over the U.K. But this also gave them the chance to try out new material on a live audience. The schedule was grueling.

On Saturday, October 5, 1968, they had to travel around London's West End to promote their single "Magic Bus" on a 100-year-old open-top green double-decker London bus with a parrot, a lion, a baby elephant, and models from the Annie Walker Agency, who had famously provided the female nudes for the sleeve of Jimi Hendrix's *Electric Ladyland*. The whole thing was filmed by Chris

Stamp. Keith Moon said, "I bet it doesn't even make the charts after this." He was right.

That night they had been booked to perform a 45-minute set in the "Middle Earth" show with the Fox and Blossom Toes at the Roundhouse, a converted tram-turning-shed in Primrose Hill, north London. They played for more than an hour and a half. The show ended with Townshend breaking his guitar over his knee, attacking it with a mike stand, and kicking his speakers off the stage.

On Monday, October 7, they flew to Bremen in Germany to record a "Magic Bus" clip for N.D.R.-T.V.'s *Beat Club*. The fee was just $90 and Keith Moon kicked over his drum set at the end of the song, wiping out any possibility of a profit.

That Friday they had to repeat the bus trip around London's West End. Then they recorded another "Magic Bus" clip for the B.B.C.'s *How It Is* at Television Centre, White City in west London. That evening they performed at York University in the north of England with Spooky Tooth. The following night that played in the University of Sheffield, Yorkshire with the Crazy World of Arthur Brown.

After another four days in the studio, they played a late-night gig at the Lyceum Balloon in London. The show did not even start until after midnight. On Saturday, they played the California Ballroom in Dunstable, Bedfordshire.

The following Friday they did another "Middle Earth" show in Leicester with the Family and Joe Cocker. Fortunately a performance for T.V. was canceled. But that Wednesday, October 30, they had to play at Eel Pie Island, Twickenham. A round of interviews followed that weekend. Then on Monday, Keith Moon, who was coming down with influenza, had to appear at Clerkenwell Magistrates Court, north London, charged with being drunk and disorderly. He was fined £2 ($3). Passing sentence, the magistrate said, "Now we don't want you playing in the traffic any more, Mr. Moon."

"Absolutely," said Keith. "They already have a drummer."

They were back in the studio when Chris Welch of *Melody Maker*—also known as *M.M.*—turned up with a copy of his august magazine. Leafing through it, Daltrey came across a reader's letter from a Mr. D. Hutchinson of Edinburgh accusing The Who of having "sold out" and saying "the Yanks can have them."

"That's a nasty letter," said Daltrey menacingly. "What's that all about?"

"Roger looked as though he might rip the *M.M.* in half at any instant, dash out, and institute a personal search for the author and possibly strangle him with the chain he habitually wears around his throat," said Welch.

Instead he simply contented himself with "growled imprecations," which, had they been audible above the dull thump of Keith Moon's nine-unit drum set a couple of rooms away, "were doubtless of a forceful character."

Welch said that Pete Townshend and John Entwistle wore expressions of aggressive indifference when they heard about the content of the letter.

"While they made it clear that they would not be distracted from the work in the studio to seek out the detractor, they clutched their guitars in such a way that, should he suddenly appear in their midst by some quirk of fate, there would be no hesitation on their part in breaking their instruments over his head."

The Who's resentment at such criticism was understandable, as most fans and critics agreed that the band was now at the peak of its creativity. Welch said that, as people, the band members had mellowed and rounded. However, "their ability too react to people and situations with lightning speed remains, with sharp eyes and tongues at the ready to encourage honesty, or crucify stupidity."

Welch wrote about the studio visit in the *Melody Maker* of November 9, 1968. In the piece, he did not mention *Tommy* by name, but he did say that the band were recording, "Pete Townshend's pop opera, a project that he has been talking about for years." And there is no doubting about the importance of task. The Who were, the headline announced, "Tackling the most serious project of their lives."

After Keith, Pete, and John had laid down a few backing tracks, the entire band, plus co-manager Kit Lambert, took a break at the nearby pub with Welch.

"The L.P. is about a deaf, dumb, and blind boy..." Pete began to explain to Welch over a pint of flat English beer. But their conversation was then drowned out by Kit Lambert's raucous laugh. Welch cupped his hands over his ear to catch what Townshend was saying, "... a deaf, dumb, and blind boy who's maltreated as a youngster," he continued, "who develops his consciousness. When he does get his sight and hearing back at the age of 22, he becomes a divine, beautiful figure who is idolized by millions."

Townshend imparted more of the storyline.

"As a kid a lot of things happen to him. His homosexual uncle who is supposed to be looking after him rapes him, for example. But none of these things worries him too much."

While the rest of the band were sharing a joke, Townshend, Welch noticed, was in deadly earnest.

"The music is coming together and sounds very good," he told Welch. "We want to try and get it out before Christmas…" In fact the release date of the album was still six months way.

Then Townshend said it.

"… It is the most serious project we have ever worked on."

But nothing with The Who was ever that serious. Back at the studio Pete and Keith struggled to uncork a bottle of wine. When they finally succeed, the two of them did a little dance. The young technicians in charge of the eight-track recording machine in the control room above them looked down imperiously. It was time to get back to work.

In the afternoon session, Pete abandoned the guitar for the piano for one track. Welch remarked that he had a "most violent, funky touch—rather like a cross between Lil Armstrong and Crippled Clarence Lofton." That is jazz-pianist Lil Hardin Armstrong, the second wife of Louis Armstrong, who used to record with him in the 1920s, and the legendary "rent party" boogie pianist Cripple Clarence Lofton.

Townshend also made quite a few mistakes and had to make frequent stops.

"If Pete makes a mistake, carry on," said the engineer, "so John doesn't have to keep doing it."

Afterward, Townshend took over control of the desk, getting the balance right and improving the drum sound. It was clear to Welch that Townshend had an advanced grasp of the technical side of recording.

While Pete was working on the control desk, Welch got to speak with John Entwistle.

"I've written a couple of songs for the opera," he said. "People might say it's sick, but it's not really. It's got a very happy ending."

Already they had been recording for about three weeks.

"Roger is singing the main parts," said Entwistle, "while me and Pete sing harmonies behind him, all the oohs and ahs. Success in the States has really pulled us together and everybody gets on well with everybody nowadays."

Although the new album was far from finished, The Who were contractually obliged to go out on the "Magic Bus" U.K. tour. It was part of a package with Joe Cocker, the Small Faces, and the Crazy World of Arthur Brown. So they had to take two weeks off recording.

The first show was at Walthamstow Granada theater in northeast London on November 8, 1968. The sound-check was at 10.30 a.m. and there was a dress rehearsal at 1.30 p.m. The 7 p.m. show found The Who far below their best form. As they trooped back to the dressing room after the first show they had long faces and Townshend was "murderous." Keith Moon complained to a journalist that the reviews of the tour had not been very good so far—they had only just finished playing the first house. The song "Magic Bus," particularly, had not gone over well and Daltrey said that The Who would now prefer to be known as an "album group."

It was pointed out that this was not the case. Albums had never worked for them in the past.

"*Quick One* [*Happy Jack* in the U.S.] was the nearest we got to something good," Daltrey admitted over a drink, "and live albums are not good"—they had recorded at the Fillmore East—"because there is so much leaping about on stage and it wouldn't come over. But the next album we hope will be it."

Then they went back on stage for the second house and played a blinder. The band were frenzied. While The Who were playing an extended version of "Magic Bus," Moon split this trousers and tore his shirt and Townshend smashed his guitar into the floor and rammed it into a speaker. Appalled, the booking manager of the Granada circuit, John Arm, pulled the curtain on them.

"I closed the curtains because I get a bit tired of violence on stage," said Arm. "It's not necessary. I've told The Who that before. They say violence is a big part of their act in America, but I said what they do in America is one thing, and what they do in England is entirely different."

Fortunately one of The Who's roadies was quick-witted enough to snatch the line from Arm and force the curtains open again for the demolition-derby finale. The finish was a triumph—destroying microphones, guitars, amplifiers, and the drum set.

The next night they did two shows in Slough, Berkshire, with Free doing the warm-up. Then on Sunday they did two shows in Bristol. Tuesday saw them in Nottingham. Friday was taken up with filming for the B.B.C. There were two more shows—one at 10.30 p.m. and one at 6 a.m.—for the next two nights, back at the Roundhouse. On Sunday they performed two shows in Birmingham. On Monday, there were two shows in Newcastle. On Tuesday, there were two shows in Liverpool. Then on Thursday, they performed "Magic Bus" on a children's T.V. show at the B.B.C. They had not resorted to such desperate measures to promote a single before. Then there was another session for *How It Is*, the next day, followed by a concert in St Albans, Hertfordshire.

Despite this grueling schedule, on November 16, 1968, *New Musical Express—N.M.E.*—reported that The Who— "possibly the last of the late great British groups (saving the enormous potential of the Small Faces) who remain to face us 'live' from the stage—had finished the tracks of the new album, still provisionally named *Deaf, Dumb and Blind Boy*." This was somewhat premature.

N.M.E. were already convinced that it was "likely to give the group an entirely new significance." Gone, the magazine said, were the guitar-smashing bunch of the past five years. And this change of direction—and the band's continued success—was "largely due to the tall bony figure of Pete Townshend, who cares so intensely about what he is doing."

The author of the 1965 youth anthem "My Generation" and "Magic Bus" then told the paper, "I can not longer sit down with a straight face and write things like that, although I was quite serious about it at the time... Mind you, I still don't know what 'Magic Bus' is all about."

The article explained that the band were in a quandary about where to go next in their recording career after suddenly finding success as a touring band in the U.S.

"'Magic Bus' was at a time when we had just returned from our first [sic] trip to America, having been conned left, right, and center," said Townshend, "and no one really wanted to make a single except Kit Lambert, whose job was to that see that we did. We got absolutely paralytic drunk one lunch time and by the time we arrived at the studio no one cared what we did."

Many have spotted the influence of the Beatles' *Magical Mystery Tour*, released the previous year, but an outline of the song may have been written before that. Townshend said, "'Magic Bus' was just a lot of fun—Keith bashing about and 'Jes' from the Alan Bown Set singing in that Stevie Winwood-type voice on the record. We were just enjoying ourselves."

The problem was that Townshend had no more singles up his sleeve.

"It's very difficult to know just what is going to be a hit for us now," he told journalist Keith Altham, "especially in America where, we weren't able to do those discs like 'Happy Jack,' 'Pictures of Lily,' and 'I'm a Boy,' which were novelty hits in England because they had the strange attraction of being 'sweet songs' sung by a violent group. In America we have to find instant hits and that's really what 'Magic Bus' is."

Sadly, peaking at number 25 in the U.S. and number 26 in the U.K., that was exactly what it wasn't.

Altham noted that Townshend was holding an old movie poster of *Gone with the Wind* in one hand—which he "sacrilegiously referred to as 'that cowboy picture'"—and a pint of beer in the other, as he launched into a long diatribe about the pop-music station Radio One.

Altham conceded that Townshend was, "incredibly easy to interview, although his deeper philosophical ideas often weigh down his arguments and you find yourself lost in a sea of imponderables." *Rolling Stone* had the same problem. The previous month Townshend had given an interview where he became, "so heavy that he almost sank under this own intellectual weight and the inner man lay bare and almost embarrassingly vulnerable."

"They really had me over a barrel with that interview," Townshend admitted. "Everything just came spilling out—sometimes I get so involved I wish I could preserve Keith's humorous approach to matters, I say about ten paragraphs and he comes along and destroys it all with one lunatic word."

Keith Richards once wrote to Townshend after a particularly pretentious interview, saying simply, "shut up."

Altham said that Townshend was "almost frighteningly involved" in the new album, still entitled *Deaf, Dumb and Blind Boy*. Townshend, he said, had been working on it for nearly two years and, "has obviously thought long and deeply over the problems." Altham merely comments, "It is a far-from-'sick' subject, although too much attention to the subject might make it so."

Then Townshend explained his intentions.

"I wanted to get an appreciation of things through the eyes of someone or something that was not preconditioned by the bias of the senses," he said. "I thought of looking at life through the eyes of animals, adolescents and finally the deaf, dumb, and blind boy. The boy registers everything in the form of musical vibration. That is, if he is struck a blow—he does not feel pain—he experiences something like the chord of G. In the beginning, he is abused by his family, raped by an uncle, and given drugs like L.S.D. to help his condition."

Still some six months away from its release—and still called *Deaf, Dumb and Blind Boy*—it was clear that *Tommy*'s storyline was now fully formed.

"Because of his disabilities, he develops a technique which enables him to become a pinball-playing champion," said Townshend. "His sight begins to come back and he becomes obsessed by his own reflection in the mirror—then his hearing is restored when his mother shatters the mirror. He finally ends up as a kind of national hero who lectures on his disabilities and how he overcame them—a kind of cross between Billy Graham and a rock-and-roll star. He founds a holiday camp (this is Moon's idea) where all the people try to become like him by wearing eye patches, ear plugs, and having corks in their mouths."

Despite Townshend's earnest art-school intentions, it was plain that he could not get away with too much intellectualizing in front of the working-class Daltrey, Moon, and Entwistle.

"In a way I am mocking myself because the album contains ideas and attitudes which are very important to me personally and, by placing them in front of The Who, they have destroyed them," he said. "It helps you put something in perspective sometimes if you can take something you really care about and laugh at it."

Townshend then said that he had no faith in science or evolution, but he believed that the album might help him achieve some sort of "divinity."

While Daltrey eschewed any religious reflections, he was impressed with the progress Townshend had made.

"He's been talking about it for so long, people think he's all mouth," Daltrey said, "but he's really written some fantastic stuff. For while it seemed he was up against a brick wall and his writing was at a standstill. Now suddenly he has soared above it and got it all together."

Another thing that had put *Tommy* into perspective was getting out on the road again in England.

The Who in the late Sixties: (left to right) Keith Moon, Pete Townshend, Roger Daltrey, and John Entwistle

The Isle of Wight Festival which was staged in 1968, 1969, and 1970 became the nearest thing Britain had to its own Woodstock. The pictures of The Who on this page and opposite were taken when they appeared at the 1969 event.

Roger Daltrey

Pete Townshend

The band took the Isle of Wight stage on Satuday August 30, having appeared at Woodstock itself just two weeks earlier.

John Entwistle

Keith Moon

In the recording studio in September 1968 (left to right) Entwistle, Daltry, Townshend, and manager Kit

Pete Townshend looking pensive, listening to a playback at the same recording session.

Meher Baba, whose philosophy had a big influence on Pete Townshend during the heady years of the late Sixties.

Townshend was also fascinated by the writings of George Adamski who claimed to have had first-hand encounters with aliens who had visited the earth in "flying saucer" spacecraft.

Daltrey, with Keith Moon in the background, on stage at the legendary Woodstock Festival in August 1969.

The back cover of a bootleg album of Tommy Live at the Rainbow, recorded in London on September 12, 1972.

*A still from the Tommy movie, with Hollywood
actress Ann-Margret as Nora Walker Hobbs and
Oliver Reed playing her husband Frank Hobbs.*

*On stage at the Shaftesbury Theatre, London,
Kim Wilde as Nora and Paul Keating as Tommy
in the revival of 'The Who's Tommy' in 1996.*

"You tend to forget what it's all about if you stop appearing on stage," said Townshend. "You work in a recording studio with instruments and all the technical hang-ups and then go out and face an audience in somewhere like Newcastle and it soon comes home. Someone recently wrote how good our act was and what a great guitarist I was—personally I think I'm just a flash ****."

And throughout the fall, the gigs kept coming. They even took time off from recording to spend 18 hours filming for *The Rolling Stones' Rock and Roll Circus* in early December, before flying to Paris to record a four-hour T.V. special.

Despite the intense pressure, the band worked well together. Gone were the arguments, the fights, and the histrionics that had marked recording sessions earlier their career. Although Townshend must be credited with the concept and the preliminary work, in the studio producing *Tommy* became a genuine team effort.

Pete Townshend recalled the recording of *Tommy* as a particularly happy time. Between sessions they all hung out in the pub together. Once Townshend had managed to jettison the opera's pretentious ending, thanks to Keith Moon's suggestion of setting it in a holiday camp, he knew they were on track.

Moon's drumming was as spectacular as ever. Entwistle's embellishment with French horn and trumpet added the appropriate classical tone and Daltrey's singing was more fiery, clear, and self-assured than ever before.

"You known, Keith, we have a huge hit on our hands," Townshend told Moon at the pub.

Moon simply said, "Good."

Other visitors to the studio included the photographers Barrie Wentzell and Baron Welman. They were surprised to find the band mellow, calm, and hard-working—nothing like the image they had in the press.

"The energy and the vibes in the studio were magnificent," recalled Chris Stamp. "Kit was prowling around with a Players Navy Cut [cigarette] always hanging out of his mouth, the tail of his white shirt always hanging out of the back of his trousers, trying to make a four-piece band sound like a symphony orchestra."

Lambert was the man who kept the show on the road.

"Kit knew the value of burning studio time," said Townshend. "He knew the value of saying, 'Right, there's too many takes, they're getting worse; everybody over to the pub.' Pick everybody up and take them out and perhaps not go back to the studio all night. You'd go home feeling terrible, and you'd think, "Oh, we've had a terrible day and why did Kit take us out.' But next day you go in and do that track straight away because you've built up to do it overnight and you get this great recording. He knew about techniques like that; he knew human nature and he knew The Who."

The atmosphere in the studio was so harmonious that Kit Lambert even had time to sit down during the sessions and write a movie script around the story, called *Tommy 1914— 1984*, which he showed the band. This was an essential part of the development of the album. Chris Stamp recalled that Lambert had written it at a time when the project, "was falling all over the place, it was just not coming together." He then had it, "printed up as a script to impress the group."

Although this had been done to keep the storyline of the album on track, the script soon had a life of its own. In January 1969, The Who announced that they planned to create a made-for-T.V. movie of *Deaf, Dumb and Blind Boy*—along the lines of the Beatles' T.V. movie, *Magical Mystery Tour*, which had been shown on the B.B.C. on December 26, 1967, although it was released as a feature film in the U.S. Unfortunately *Magical Mystery Tour* had had a drubbing from fans and critics alike in the U.K. and Townshend railed against any possibly censorship that his work might suffer in the hands of the broadcasters.

Besides, the album was still not finished. On January 21 and 22, there were more sessions at I.B.C., although these had to be squeezed in between gigs and interviews. Meanwhile Townshend was producing and playing the bass on four "Thunderclap" Newman tracks.

On February 1, 1969, The Who announced that they were about to release Pete Townshend's "Pinball Wizard"—the first track from the new album—as a single. A release date had not been fixed yet, but it was coming out within the next four weeks. *Deaf, Dumb and Blind Boy* would also be released in a few weeks' time and would now be a double album.

"They had recorded so much good material that it has been decided to release a double album under the same title," a spokesman for the group said. In addition, an eight-week coast-to-coast U.S. tour promoting the album would kick off on *The Ed Sullivan Show*, on May 8.

Double studio albums were rare beasts back them. In 1966, Bob Dylan had produced *Blonde on Blonde* as a double album and the Mothers of Invention had released *Freak Out* in that format. There followed a spate of double albums in 1968 and 1969, including *The Beatles* [the White Album], Jimi Hendrix's *Electric Ladyland*, Cream's *Wheels of Fire*, Chicago's *Chicago Transit Authority*, and Frank Zappa's *Uncle Meat*. Releasing a double album meant that The Who would be putting themselves among rock's elite.

There were further recording sessions at I.B.C. from February 3 to 7, and again from February 10 to 14. *Rolling Stone* then blithely announced that the album *Deaf, Dumb and Blind Boy* was finally finished on February 15, 1969. It was not true. There were further sessions at I.B.C. from February 17 to 21, from February 24 to 28 and March 3 to March 7. Again these sessions were squeezed in between gigs all over the U.K.

And still no one was happy with the title. Townshend's rock opera had variously been called *The Brain Opera* and *Journey into Space* along the way. In March, Kit Lambert announced that the album had now been retitled *Tommy, 1914—1984* and that the band would be interested in turning it into a full-length feature film.

Although it was originally envisaged that the recording would take under two months, recording only finished on March 7, 1969. Daltrey reckoned it took, "only about eight weeks in the studio." However, that studio time had been stretched out over 24 weeks.

Once recording was finished, Kit Lambert took off for a holiday in Egypt, leaving Damon Lyon-Shaw and his assistant Ted Sharp struggling with the final mixing in Studio B at I.B.C.

"Studio B at I.B.C. was not a good studio to mix the album," said Lyon-Shaw. "We never knew what was wrong with it, and Kit left it to us to finish it off."

In all, the album had cost £40,000 ($60,000) to produce. This was considered a huge amount in those days. Even then it was not really finished. The band thought that it required many more overdubs, including a new guitar track. Some tracks remained rough and unpolished.

"It was at the time very un-Who-like," said Moon. "A lot of the songs were soft. We never played like that."

Townshend was not displeased by this.

"When you listen to the early stuff, it's incredibly raucous and high energy," he said. "But this was fairly laid back, and Kit deliberately mixed it like that, with the voices up front. The music was structured to allow the concept to breathe."

Even though they had decided to make the opera into a double album halfway through the sessions, so that the storyline could unfold naturally without vital plot points being excised, some tracks just had to be cut. Mose Allison's "Young Man Blues" was recorded and, though it was dropped from *Tommy*, it appeared on the Tracks' artists' sampler album *The House That Track Built* in 1969. However, the song became a regular part of The Who's stage act and finally caught up with *Tommy* again as a bonus track included on the Deluxe 5.1 Surround Sound CD in 2003. The recording of Mercy Dee's "One Room Country Shack" was abandoned at the time and has never resurfaced.

Townshend had planned to record three more songs to help the story along. They were called "Success," "Beat Up," and "Girl From Lincoln County." Dave Davis released a single called "Lincoln County" in 1968, which may have been related. But these songs never made it into the studio. Way past their deadline, The Who had to stop. New commitments beckoned. They were booked on a new tour to promote the album, even though it was not yet finished.

The final stereo mastering of *Tommy* was done in Studio A at I.B.C. during the week of April 21 and interest in the long-awaited album had now reached fever pitch. But Keith Moon immediately poured cold water on it. In a short interview in *Hit Parader* magazine on April 23, he blithely announcing, "Our albums are junk." This was a typical piece of Moon mischief-making. The Who's real talent, he said, lay in smashing up hotel rooms. During the interview, Moon repeatedly ran into the offices of *Amateur Gardener*, which adjoined those of *Hit Parader*, and yelled, "Weeds." Moon also denied that The Who fell into the category of such high-concept bands as the Doors. Nevertheless *Melody Maker* had already promoted them to the "heavy mob" alongside such bands as Free and Led Zeppelin.

With the album now finished, the storyline and running order had finally been settled. It began with the "Overture"— standard practice in an opera, but revolutionary on a rock album. As in classical operas, this is a collection of instrumental themes snatched from the songs that follow— notably "Pinball Wizard," "We're Not Gonna Take It," and "See Me Feel Me." These are linked together by the bass riff from "Go To The Mirror." Melodic touches were added by John Entwistle on the French horn and the guitar parts were played by Pete Townshend on an acoustic Gibson J-200. It runs to five minutes 20 seconds. Towards the end, the organ comes in with the "Listening To You" melody from "See Me Feel Me." Then, alone with an acoustic guitar, Townshend begins the story, "Captain Walker didn't come home...." He had been posted missing in action during World War I—which, for Britain, lasted from 1914 to 1918.

Although World War II was fresher in the national psyche in both Britain and America—indeed three members of The Who had been born while it was still going on—the initial action of *Tommy* was shifted back in time to World War I for a good reason. At the time Britain and America were fiercely proud of their victory in the war against Nazism. The sacrifices made to defeat Hitler's Germany and Tojo's Japan were fresh in everyone's minds, putting World War II out of bounds as a subject even for a strident young rock band. However, the controversial musical, *Oh What A Lovely War*, mocking the British involvement in World War I, had come to the London stage in 1963.

Richard Attenborough's movie version of *Oh What A Lovely War* would come out the same year as *Tommy* the album. Its action is largely set on a seaside pier. The movie *Tommy* was to follow suit, until their chosen pier, at Southsea on the English south coast, burned down. In the movie, the director Ken Russell moved the beginning to World War II, thus making Tommy roughly the same age as The Who and their fans.

A four-note phrase on the French horn signals the end of the "Overture" and Townshend's strumming leads into "It's A Boy." This is sung in a high register by Townshend and, in just 38 seconds, it announces Tommy's birth. Again Townshend's acoustic guitar leads into "1921"—which was called "You Didn't Hear It" in the U.S. In it, we are assured that 1921 is "going to be a good year." But it is not to be. Tommy's mother has taken a lover and, in 1921, Captain

Walker finally returns from the war. He finds his wife with another man and kills him. It is a melodic ballad sung, again, by Townshend.

But Tommy has witnessed the crime in the mirror and the track continues, "You didn't hear it, you didn't see it, you won't say nothing to no one...." Tommy is traumatized. As his mother beats and brainwashes the child into silence, he withdraws into himself, making himself psychosomatically deaf, dumb, and blind, leaving him only with his sense of touch. At two minutes 49 seconds, "1921" is the perfect length for a pop song and was considered for release as a single.

Deprived of sensory input from the world, Tommy develops the power of his own imagination which takes him on an "Amazing Journey." This is the first true rock song on the album. Daltrey sings it in a lighter timbre, letting himself be led by Moon's drumming. The vocal is double-tracked, and behind Townshend's chord progressions, there is a tape playing backwards, giving the piece an ethereal quality. "Amazing Journey" is another stand-alone piece that was electrifying when performed on stage. It runs to five minutes four seconds and segues into the instrumental "Sparks," which continues for another two minutes seven seconds. It is here that Tommy develops his fantastic inner world, spurred by the vibrations he feels. More than a musical bridge, it introduces themes from *Rael* that will be used again five tracks later in "Underture." And it cranks up the drama of the piece, both on disc and on stage.

A traveling quack called Hawker turns up and claims that his gypsy wife can cure Tommy. He is selling "Eyesight For The Blind." This is the only song on the album that is not a

Who original. Written by Sonny Boy Williamson, it was originally called "The Hawker." Pete Townshend picked it up from a jazz cover version by Mose Allison, who was one of Townshend's musical heroes from the Sunnyside Road days. Townshend added an innovative guitar solo and, because the song directly mentions Tommy's disabilities, it sounds like it was written for the piece. The track runs to two minutes 13 seconds. Two versions of this song have appeared on various pressings of *Tommy* since 1969. The only difference between the two tracks is that in one, Daltrey's voice is an octave higher than the other.

"Christmas" is the first "Who-style" track and runs to four minutes 33 seconds. It is both upbeat and unnerving with a slightly off-key background vocal. Townshend introduces the "Tommy, can you hear me?" theme over a crashing drum roll, and running through the middle of it is Daltrey's plaintive "See Me Feel Me" motif. It tells of Tommy's parent's growing frustration and despair at the child's disabilities. They then leave him with "Cousin Kevin," the school bully who torments the disabled Tommy. Entwistle delivers the song with convincing sadism and wrote it in a key so high that Daltrey could not sing it. It runs out at four minutes four seconds.

A linking song, "Cousin Kevin Model Child"—credited to Entwistle, but actually written by Townshend and sung by Keith Moon—was recorded, but was dropped before the final mastering. It reappeared almost 30 years later on an extended version of the 1974 Who album *Odds and Sods*, which was originally produced as a home for all the tracks that The Who had recorded over the years and never released.

Townshend later explained why this and other songs had been dropped.

"There were times in *Tommy*'s later incarnations in the film and the musical where I've written new songs to serve a particular function required to help tell the story better," he said. "I had already anticipated that, and there are songs that were supposed to serve those functions. But really when we put the album together we realized that the story shouldn't be too complete, for rock and roll... there should be mystery in it and loose ends."

Daltrey saw the sense in that.

"*Tommy* came along at a time in our lives when everyone was searching for answers in their life," he said. "The ambiguity of *Tommy* allowed it to answer many things for many different people. But in fact it didn't really answer anything. That was the beauty of it."

Directly after "Cousin Kevin," the Hawker's gypsy wife, "The Acid Queen," administers her medicine, which turns out to be L.S.D. Townshend said that this song came from the fact that his family had some gypsy blood. His mad Granny Denny was the daughter of a gypsy girl. The Acid Queen was also a camped-up version of the trendy drug pushers seen around Shepherd's Bush.

At three minutes 34 seconds, "The Acid Queen" has overtly drug-oriented lyric with a strong rock melody. Townshend's vocal and the electric piano add a sultry sexiness to the mix. Townshend later explained, "The song is not just about acid. It's the whole drug thing, the drink thing, the sex thing, wrapped into one big ball. It's about how you get it laid on you if you haven't fucked 40 birds, taken

60 trips, drunk 14 pints or whatever... society—people— force it on you. She represents this force."

Tommy's trip is described musically in "Underture," another instrumental that continues the theme from "Sparks" and "Rael" on *The Who Sell Out*. In early pressings of the album, the tracks "Sparks" and "Underture" were linked by title. "Sparks" was called "Dream Sequence" and "Underture" was called "Dream Sequence (Underture)."

Townshend plays it on acoustic guitar, aided masterfully by Keith Moon.

"Moon offers up a series of emotive crescendos or otherwise doubles up on the guitar's complex rhythms, and then overdubs the whole with grandiose symphonic timpani that take the number into another dimension," says Tony Fletcher in his 588-page biography of Keith Moon, *Dear Boy*. "His rat-a-tat rolls on the snare that underscore Townshend's suspended fourth chords halfway through are potentially the definitive example of the pair's innate musical understanding; confident and unforced, they lift an already thrilling composition higher still."

Running to a massive ten minutes seven seconds—the longest track on the album—"Underture" ends the second side of the first disc, the place where in a regular opera you would have an intermission. But in The Who's stage rendition, the band plowed straight on through.

The second disc begins with Tommy's parents asking each other—and the listener—"Do You Think It's Alright?" to leave Tommy with Uncle Ernie. It is a short link of just 24 seconds. Unfortunately Uncle Ernie is a child molester who likes to "Fiddle About." This is another great vehicle for John

Entwistle's warped sense of humor. Despite its unpleasant theme and the fact that it bears little relationship to Townshend's compositions, it injects a piece of—albeit grim—humor into a work that is threatening to become too serious. Originally sung by Entwistle with a certain relish, Moon eventually took over the song on stage as it seemed to suit his manic character. Again, the track is short at just one minute 29 seconds and does not dwell in unnecessary detail on what Uncle Ernie is getting up to.

As Tommy grows older, his acute sense of touch and sensitivity to vibration allows him to become the "Pinball Wizard." In the song, Pete Townshend demonstrates his unchallenged virtuosity on the guitar. It opens with an electric riff coming in with a spine-tingling jolt over two-chord acoustic strumming. This has been compared to the opening of Richard Strauss's "Thus Spake Zarathustra," used as the title track for Stanley Kubrick's 2001: A Space Odyssey, which had been released earlier that year and was Townshend's favorite movie. His furious acoustic strumming underpins the song from the opening chords to the upward key change near the end.

On Townshend's demo the opening chord sequence runs for about 15 minutes.

"It's just an exploration of how many chords I could make with a running B," he said. "The B was in every chord. It went through about 30 or 40 chords very slowly."

Eventually it was trimmed down to nine chords played on his sweet-sounding acoustic Gibson J.-200. The progression was driven by an insistent pedal note.

"I became very interested in the drone," said Townshend. "I listened to a bit of Indian music and that influenced me, and country music has a drone through it as well. They call it bass pedal, but of course on guitar and banjo work it's not a bass, but a running note that runs through all the chords."

Consequently, the chord changes are all made with the minimum possible movement. The next chord might have three notes the same and only one different from the one before it. This gives the piece its flow. Townshend then goes into full flamenco mode. It is not until 32 seconds into the track that the first verse begins—and then only with guitar and bass accompaniment. The drums only come at the end of the verse, with the first refrain of "Sure plays a mean pinball."

The electric guitar then enters to balance the acoustic strumming on the other side of the stereo image. Townshend loved experimenting with key changes and, while the main body of the song—verses and chorus—continues in B, the bridges—"How do you think he does it?"—are in D.

At two minutes 14 seconds, the full band drops out, leaving the solo acoustic guitar which returns to the flamenco intro. Then the song begins again, this time in D, pushing Daltrey to the very top of his range. As his voice rasps and soars it still manages to convey credibly the vulnerability of an autistic adolescent.

The track is both musically and lyrically inventive—even though the idea of a deaf, dumb, and blind boy playing pinball is scarcely convincing. It is a high-energy piece that brings together the themes of Tommy's sensory deprivation, the outer world of popular culture, and idea that a Messiah could spring from such a background. Alternately mystical, squalid, obscure, fantastical, banal, and melodramatic, it was as ambitious as anything any other rock band had attempted. The track runs to three minutes 17 seconds, making it good single material.

Meanwhile his parents discover that "There's A Doctor" who might cure their son. This is a short 23-second link to the straightforward rock song "Go To The Mirror," where the specialist discovers that Tommy can see his reflection. It is a breakthrough in the therapeutic process. Again Townshend shows his mastery of composition. This time the plaintive "See Me Feel Me" and "Listening To You" are spliced into the heavy riff. "Go To The Mirror" runs to three minutes 48 seconds.

Stepping out of his roll as the deaf, dumb, and blind boy, Daltrey leads The Who in a singalong, where the band members ask in unison, "Tommy Can You Hear Me?" accompanied by John Entwistle's dancing bass line and Townshend's folksy acoustic guitar. It runs to just one minute 45 seconds.

But Tommy can't hear anyone. All he can see it his own reflection. In frustration, his mother is moved to "Smash The Mirror." This is a bluesy number and the dramatic moment is reach by the ascending lyric "rise, rise, rise," followed by the crash of breaking glass. When the mirror is smashed, Tommy's inner block is broken. Again this track is short and dramatic at one minute 23 seconds.

Then, according to the 1969/1970 tour program, "Tommy realizes the enormous powers he now has and becomes aware of his destiny as a religious leader." He is a "Sensation," with the track musically expressing Tommy's new-found freedom. Although this song had not been written with *Tommy* in mind, the lyric, after the gender change, fitted perfectly. At two minutes 28 seconds, it is a classic 1960s pop song and features Pete singing the lead vocal.

Smashing the mirror is proclaimed a "Miracle Cure" by a newspaper vendor, which offers a quick 12-second link into "Sally Simpson." She is a disciple of Tommy's, who defies her parents and heads off to see Tommy, whose powers have now made him head of an evangelical religious movement. She gets caught up in the crush at the front of the crowd and is permanently disfigured.

The song was inspired by an incident that happen on August 2, 1968 when The Who and Kangaroo were supporting the Doors at Singer Bowl in Flushing Meadow, Queens, New York. There was a sell-out crowd, but things began to go wrong from the beginning. The 50-foot revolving stage jammed, delaying the start. The Who closed the first half and, in the process, managed to smash up some of the Doors' equipment. The moment Moon threw his cymbals in the air and kicked over the drum set, while Townshend smashed his guitar into an amplifier, was caught on 8-mm color footage. This was used in the "Magic Bus" sequence in V.H.-1's *Legends: The Who*.

During the interval there was a contretemps between the roadies of The Who and the Doors over the smashed equipment. This further delayed the opening of the second half. The crowd were already restless and were goaded further by Jim Morrison's moody histrionics. Then a girl in an agitated state leaped on stage. The stagehands tried to grab her. She eluded them. But in the chase she fell off the stage and was badly injured. Townshend who was watching from the wings was both fascinated and appalled.

Musically, the song could be from a different album. It has none of the rhythmic elements found in the other tracks and the slight melody is held back to let the narrative come through. However, the incident at Spring Bowl and the song "Sally Simpson" were key elements in what inspired Townshend to write *Tommy* in the first place. It runs to four minutes 11 seconds.

Tommy celebrates discarding the shackles of his autism in "I'm Free." With it, he urges his fans—pinball fanatics everywhere—to follow his example. It is the climax of the album. Starting with an unforgettable six-chord riff, it cleverly re-uses the intro riff from "Pinball Wizard," with the pinball-playing represented this time by a tinkling piano. The track is topped off by another blinding Townshend acoustic solo. Another classic Townshend composition, it runs to two minutes 39 seconds.

Despite the sad fate of Sally Simpson, Tommy says that anyone who wants to follow him is "Welcome." Sung by Daltrey at his most melodic, its gentle, nursery-rhyme beginning cannot hold down the energy of The Who, which bursts out from all the tracks around it. It speeds up in the middle with jazz piano snatches along the lines of Dave Brubeck's "Take Five" and a blasting harmonica, before slowing to a ragged, dreamy end. Almost a mini-opera in itself, the whole thing runs to four minutes 33 seconds.

The new religion finds its home in "Tommy's Holiday Camp," the virtues of which are extolled in a one-minute vocal sung over the sound of a fairground barrel organ. This is a device stolen directly from 19th-century light opera. Townshend sings, accompanying himself on a banjo. It runs to just 57 seconds.

But in the end Tommy is then frustrated when he finds that his disciples want to opt for the easy path and follow him slavishly, rather than take a more difficult route and discover their own awareness. They reject him and destroy the holiday camp, saying, "We're Not Gonna Take It." This anti-Fascist anthem runs to three minutes 28 seconds.

The rejection of Tommy by his followers—and their rejection by him—is the saving grace of *Tommy* narratively. The rock opera could have ended with Tommy self-righteously finding the "way" and his followers accepting his wisdom. He would then have become one of those phony religious leaders the world seems so full of.

As it is Tommy finds himself isolated and removed from the world once more, but now he has achieved self-awareness. In the climax of the finale, Tommy begs the listener to "See Me Feel Me." This, according to the program, is, "Tommy's continuing statement of wonder at that which encompasses him."

Initially, the two songs were lumped under the one title "We're Not Gonna Take It," with "See Me Feel Me" considered merely a coda. But later it was acknowledged to be a song in its own right.

In fact, "See Me Feel Me" is two songs. Interweaved with it is "Listening To You," which makes it obvious that this is a prayer to Meher Baba. And like all successful hymns, it cannot fail to elevate the spirit. Together, the track now entitled "See Me Feel Me/Listening To You" runs to three minutes 32 seconds.

Once the band had heard the album through, there was some criticism of Kit Lambert's production. Entwistle said that the drums sounded "like biscuit tins" and he was annoyed upset that Lambert had rushed the band to finish the album and limited their opportunity for overdubs. Townshend announced that the sound as merely "passable."

Chris Stamp explained, "Kit was never a great ears producer. He wasn't into getting a perfect sound. He didn't know about the best place to position the mikes and all that. He was a creative and intuitive 'ideas' producer."

Lambert was hurt by these criticisms and *Tommy* would be the last record he would produce for The Who. But Townshend, for one, was grateful for his input.

"Kit's real contribution will never be known because, of course, it was not production at all, it was far deeper," said Townshend. "Kit was much more involved in the overall concept of the thing—much more than people imagine. Not all that much, in fact, with the overall sound. Although he did produce and mix it, and he did make us work at it—still the main thing was that he thought of the idea of a rock opera."

Even so, *Tommy* is a musical triumph as it seamlessly moves from track to track pushing the story forward. It also works lyrically and Townshend pulled off his early concept of shifting the point of view. Tracks alternate between the outer "objective" reality and Tommy's inner "subjective" reality. It takes the listener from the brutal certainties of the past—World War I—into some point in the, then, distant future. The early title *Tommy, 1914—1984*, seems to indicate that the story ends in 1984. Presumably this date was chosen because of George Orwell's novel, *1984*, and because it gave Tommy his biblically allotted span of three score years and ten. However, in the final version, we don't find out anything about Tommy's ultimate fate. Townshend explained that this was the fault of his "peculiar working process."

"Like often I pretend to everybody that I know what I'm doing when a lot of the time I really don't," he said. "I seem to think I do but I don't really… until things come together. That's why *Tommy* and *Quadrophenia* haven't got properly conceived endings… because they were never properly conceived in front… Rather than something that was scripted in front and made to happen, it was allowed to happen."

On the other hand, Townshend insisted that a clear ending was not needed because "drawing a conclusion is not my job."

"What I was doing at the time was attending to the fact that in rock and roll what you don't do is make people's decisions for them," he explained later, "You share their ideas and you share their difficulties and you share their periods of frustration. But you don't say 'the thing that you have to do now is get yourself a job, get a pension scheme.' You don't do that stuff. You say, 'let's go get drunk and talk about it.'"

Although the album was released with a booklet containing the lyrics that point out which character is saying which line, the narrative is never entirely clear. Even John Entwistle admitted, "When we were recording the damn thing, nobody knew what it was all about or how the hell it was going to end… I had absolutely no idea what the story was, who the characters were or what they did."

But then, the plotlines of operas rarely make much sense. It is only one of the elements that give the piece a musical and emotional cohesion.

"It works on so many different levels," said Townshend. "And with something this big you can't control it... What really should happen is for me to entertain and illustrate something which is going to make their lives more pleasant."

The Who knew, of course, that they were wide open to the accusation of pretentiousness. That is why they decided to release "Pinball Wizard"—as the hardest, most commercial, most Mod-inspired, most Who-like track—as the first single. It was also a deliberate ploy to soften up the U.S. market. By that time Nik Cohn had a column in *The New York Times*. He was a pop purist and deeply suspicious of concept albums, rock operas, and any other sign that rock musicians were getting above themselves. But because he was a pinball fan, The Who knew that he would give "Pinball Wizard" a good review. The single is a slightly speeded-up version of the album track, making it more hard-edged, more exciting and more Who-like.

"Pinball Wizard" was released in the U.K. on March 7, the day the album was finished, with "Dogs Part 2" on the B-side, which was attributed to "Moon, Towser, Jason"—Towser and Jason were Townshend and Entwistle's dogs who are heard barking on the track—in the U.K. In the U.S., Moon alone was credited, presumably because of the difficulty of paying royalties to animals.

In the U.K., "Pinball Wizard" drew immediate criticism. The Who had had an uneasy relationship with the B.B.C. since, four years earlier, the Corporation had found "My Generation" offensive to stutterers. Now B.B.C. D.J. Tony Blackburn denounced their song about a "deaf, dumb and blind kid, who could sure play a mean pinball" as "distasteful" and "sick" on his Radio One program. Most people agreed that a song about an autistic child who could play pinball was about as bizarre as you could get. The Who defended themselves, saying that the single did not give a full enough picture of what *Tommy* was about, and they sent out a press release to influential figures imploring them to reserve judgment.

The executives at Decca were less than impressed, too.

"We told them that they were going to have a 5,000,000-copy album on their hands," said Townshend.

By his own account, he was stomping around the record company, grabbing the people by the lapels and saying, "Look, this album is going to sell more copies than any other f***ing album in history so get your f***ing brains together."

Gradually "Pinball Wizard" rose to number four in the U.K.—eventually climbing to number 19 in the U.S. after its release on July 6. Critics acknowledged it was the best thing The Who had done since "I Can See For Miles" and showed unfaltering inspiration and originality.

"It is a work of pure genius," Penny Valentine wrote in *Disc and Music Echo* on March 8, 1969. "It also shows [that] The Who, brilliant bunch that they are, improve all the time."

Decca executives then began to take *Tommy* seriously. The problem was that the album now faced the stiff competition in the record stores. *Tommy* had taken so long to produce when it was released in the U.K. on May 23, 1968—a week earlier in the U.S.—it found itself up against the Small Faces' *Ogden's Nut Gone Flake*, the Kinks' *The Village Green Preservation Society*, and the Pretty Things *S.F. Sorrow*. Even so, *Tommy* was about to make its mark.

Disc and Music Echo called *Tommy*, "A masterpiece... The Who, as a magnificent group, project the story brilliantly in music."

The U.K. underground magazine *It*, financed by the Beatle Paul McCartney, said, "It is impossible to praise this album too highly... The Who have pulled together the threads of rock and roll, progressive pop, social comment and present philosophical developments till they have crystallized into this one project—a massive undertaking... The Who are ahead of everyone!"

Even *The New York Times'* Albert Goldman—later the author of controversial biographies of Elvis Presley and John Lennon—said that work was breakthrough, both for opera and for rock and roll.

But the praise was not universal. Some found *Tommy's* content unsettling.

The *New Musical Express* headlined its record review, "Who's Sick Opera." The reviewer went on to say that the album was "a disappointment... pretentious is too strong a word; maybe over-ambitious is the right term, but sick certainly does apply."

The following week, the *N.M.E.'s* rival *Melody Maker* struck back with a rave from Chris Welch, headlined, "An Extremely Tasteful Opera." Later the *Melody Maker* named *Tommy* "album of the year."

Jazz & Pop nitpicked, complaining that, "*Tommy* is not an opera. A real opera is acted as well as sung; it has well-defined parts and *recitative* and many other characteristics. *Tommy* is a rock cantata: in other words, a piece of music which is primarily vocal—a sung piece... although *Tommy* could easily be seen called a "Passion" in the traditional sense. In many senses, Tommy's journey to realization is very like Christ's."

In *The New York Times*, Nik Cohn was similarly thoughtful about the album.

"Townshend is intelligent, creative, highly complex, and much given to mystic ponderings," he wrote, "but the things that he values most in rock are its basic explosions, its noise and flash and image... So he writes stuff like *Tommy*, sophisticated as it is, and he can see that it's good but, at the same time, he feels that it's a cop-out from all the things that rock lives off, almost a betrayal. And he goes out on stage and he smashes his guitar as, simple, mindless release."

playing **Tommy**

Although the album was now completed, The Who still had to learn how to play *Tommy* on stage, but rehearsals were interrupted by a round of interviews and TV appearances to plug "Pinball Wizard." The fate of the whole album, they felt, depended on the success of the single.

On Friday, March 14, before a gig at the Corn Exchange in Cambridge, they rehearsed and taped "Pinball Wizard" at B.B.C. Television Centre for an unbilled appearance on *How Late It Is*, a late-night music show. There were more rehearsals on March 18, but these were interrupted by a live interview on the B.B.C. pop show *Radio One Club*.

Rehearsals began in earnest the following Wednesday, with the band hard at work in Bickersteth Memorial Hall in Hampstead, north London from 1 p.m. to around 6.30 each day. But they had other commitments. The following day they had to mime to a pre-recorded version of "Pinball Wizard" on the long-running U.K. T.V. pop show, *Top of the Pops*. The B.B.C. also used this tape to broadcast abroad.

The next day, The Who had to play live on London's Thames T.V.'s *Today* show. Townshend's first daughter, Kate, was also born that day. The following Monday, they were back in the studio in Denmark Street in the West End of London, taking a quick break for publicity shots on the roof.

Rehearsals took place in the Community Centre in Hanwell, west London, on April 1, 3, 8, 9, 10, 11, 21, and 23. One of these full rehearsals, or possibly one from later in the year, was taped as a reference and cut as a set of single-sided acetates. These rehearsals were punctuated with gigs in Bournemouth, Dorset, and Bolton, Lancashire. They also shot a performance of "Pinball Wizard" for the T.V. show *This Is... Tom Jones*, which went out on A.B.C. in the U.S. on April 18 and on the commercial I.T.V. network in the U.K. on April 20. Townshend recorded a radio interview for the B.B.C., part of which appeared on the *Live At The BBC* bonus disc released in the U.S. in February, 2000.

Another appearance on *Top Of The Pops* on April 10 was disrupted by the misbehavior of Keith Moon, much to the annoyance of the show's director. The B.B.C. added a new clause to The Who's appearance contract. Next time the band were to ensure that their drummer remained sober for the whole of the day. It did no good. Two weeks later their appearance on *Top Of The Pops* playing "Pinball Wizard" was introduced by Tony Blackburn. Moon took his revenge for the things the D.J. had said about the single by flicking drum sticks at him, live on air.

The day before, The Who had had a final rehearsal of *Tommy* at Hanwell Community Centre. Afterwards, Townshend and Moon went to the pub to discuss where *Tommy* was taking them.

"We sat there incredulous at how quickly it had come together," said Townshend. "We noted how suddenly Roger had become something else, and we debated what would happen, and how it would change everything. We knew we had something cohesive and playable and that had a story."

On Friday, April 25, for the first time, The Who tried out an extensive rendering of *Tommy* before an audience at

Glasgow's Strathclyde University in Scotland. They played two more gigs in Scotland, then one in Sunderland, in the northeast of England. The aim was to try out the material on stage while keeping *Tommy* hundreds of miles from London. The Who were holding back for an official international debut of the album in the capital later that week.

On May 1, 1969, the press and pop industry were invited along to Ronnie Scott's Club—a famous jazz venue in London's Soho. At 6 p.m., the surrounding pubs and clubs emptied for what was to be a "hair-raising curtain-raiser" to the release of the double album, two years in making and now, finally, entitled simply *Tommy*. The reception was less than rapturous. When the band came on stage, they were greeted with cries of "**** off" from members of the press, many of whom were already drunk.

The Who had plied the journalists with drink deliberately. They had already been stung by criticism that "Pinball Wizard"—indeed, the entire content of the album— was "sick." Journalists, they knew, ran on booze. They were also going to get an unforgettable show. Enormous speakers, better suited to the stadium show, were stacked up against the walls of the tiny club. They hummed ominously as Pete Townshend grabbed a microphone.

"There is a story to the music," he said. "It's the story of Tommy, a boy who is born normal, just like you and me. Tommy is born at the advent of World War I. His father goes off to fight. Meanwhile, Tommy's mother takes a lover. One day Tommy sees something he shouldn't. He witnesses a murder and is told to keep quiet about it. The shock causes him to go deaf, dumb, and blind."

He was interrupted by cries of "sick!" "sick!"

"No, it's not sick, ha, ha," said Townshend, "contrary to what one hears on Auntie"—Brits' affectionate sobriquet for the B.B.C.—"I think Auntie is the sickest thing in this country."

Moon noisily seconded that opinion and there was a round of applause.

"He is later raped by his uncle," Townshend continued, "and, in the next scene, gets turned on to L.S.D., as has been explained in various in-depth interviews, by a gypsy, the Acid Queen, who declares that she will take him into a room for a while and make a man out of the boy. Following this episode Tommy becomes the renowned 'Pinball Wizard.'"

Townshend explained how the young boy's handicaps equipped him to play pinball. Then he is healed, and becomes a hero for the younger generation. The U.K. music weekly *Record Mirror* said, "The L.P. ends with what appears to be a musical philosophical question: what happens to Tommy after his disturbed childhood? Where went the Pinball Wizard?"

The Who then played an hour-long set, covering the highlights of the album, which left most of the audience deaf—if not dumb and blind. The noise from the huge speakers was so intense in the confined space that one journalist complained that his ears were still ringing 20 hours after the event.

Despite the discomfort of those sitting directly in front of the speakers, no one left during the performance—even when the band switched from playing Townshend's original material to their revved up versions of rock classics "Shakin' All Over" and "Summertime Blues."

The audience may have been deafened, but no one could be blind to The Who's showmanship—with Daltrey whirling the microphone by its lead like a cowboy with a lasso, Townshend leaping around with his guitar and Moon drumming like a demon. Nor were they dumb when it came to praise.

The *Record Mirror* said, "The Who gave us a solid hour's worth of quality listening and excellent showmanship, leaving amid chortles of 'more!' and 'get off!' and 'to the bar!' All in all it was a great pop-religious happening and [all] ends of the scale from Dave Dee to John Peel turned up to urge the play on. Then the pubs became enormously popular once again."

The *Melody Maker* called the album's debut simply, "Pete Townshend's triumph."

Townshend's flair for inventive lyrics, his composition, his humor, and his sense of the dramatic all came in for praise. With "Pinball Wizard" riding high in the U.K. charts, critics were expecting slew of other singles from the double album which, at £23 ($35), was also praised as, "real value for money, unlike many recent doubles." *Tommy*, it was said, marked nothing less than The Who's "Renaissance." *Disc* declared *Tommy* to be a "masterpiece."

Daltrey was delighted with the reaction.

"We're really pleased about everything at the moment," he said. "I think Pete's opera is incredible. It's been a long time coming, it's true."

Daltrey said he as also knocked out with the reaction to the single "Pinball Wizard."

"It's about the most commercial song on the album," he said. "I suppose it's about our biggest hit since 'Happy Jack,' isn't it?"

However, he admitted that he had not really got used to singing the material.

"Some of the songs on the album are bloody hard. They take a lot of concentration to remember, with all the key changes and breaks. I can't say I enjoy singing them yet."

And he had some words of criticism for Townshend.

"Pete's lyrics are really getting ridiculous. Some of the things he is doing are unbelievable."

Audiences would not agree with Daltrey, especially when The Who and *Tommy* reached the U.S. There, the lyrics would draw critical acclaim. However, Daltrey conceded that Townshend and *Tommy* were putting The Who back on top.

"The last six months, it's been like the rebirth of The Who," he said. "I suppose in the early days we were too far ahead of the time and now audiences are catching up. We've calmed down a lot. Our act hasn't calmed down, at all. I mean, we have changed as people. That's what makes everything so good."

Townshend, however, was more cynical about the press reaction.

"We pandered, absolutely, to the main spice of the journalist's life," he said. "We hired a club and we gave them free booze and we entertained them so the reviews were ecstatic... generally. There were a few exceptions. There were people who found it pretentious. There were people who found the whole thing distasteful, but it was all spectacular news, whatever it was... some people hated it, some people loved it, but everybody spoke very loudly about it."

The U.K. press's reaction was, at that point, academic. *Tommy* had already missed its April release date because of problems with the manufacture of the double album's triptych sleeve and the 12-page booklet that accompanied it. This was to have contained Mike McInnerney's paintings and a synopsis of the story by Kit Lambert. In the end the booklet contained McInnerney's paintings, the album's lyrics, and four pages of full-color photographs. The original booklet was supposed to be a "limited edition" and those that came with the first pressing were numbered. However, the libretto continued to be issued with subsequent pressings, although later editions were unnumbered. As it was *Tommy* did not reach the record stores in the U.K. until May 23.

The day after the preview, Daltrey, Entwistle, and Moon flew to New York. Townshend, who was in the first flush of fatherhood, followed a few days later. He stocked up on guitars at Manny's on West 48th Street and set off on the first of two U.S. tours they would make that year to stir up interest in "Pinball Wizard" and *Tommy*.

First came a three-night stand with Joe Cocker and the Grease Band at the Grande Ballroom in Detroit, Michigan. This legendary venue was now being run by Townshend's old friend from Ealing Art School, Tom Wright, who had been a roadie on The Who's first U.S. tour in 1967 and later became their tour manager. He recorded the set on his portable Nagra tape recorder.

Being on stage with *Tommy* took Daltrey to new heights.

"You have to understand for me *Tommy* was an absolute dream," he said. "When the whole thing came together and we started performing it on stage all of a sudden I almost found myself within it. It was an amazing catalyst for me."

"He went from tough, muscled front man of The Who to

angel with curly hair," said Keith Altham. "That was down to his photographer cousin, and it fitted Tommy to a T."

It was a part Daltrey was to play for the next five years.

"People thought I was Tommy," he said. "I used to get called Tommy in the street."

After the Grande Ballroom, Detroit, they played three nights at The Boston Tea Party in Boston, Massachusetts. Then they moved on to the Fillmore East in New York City where they were booked to play the weekend starting May 16. However, the show ran into trouble the first night. The owner of the grocery store next door had refused to pay protection money to the local hoods, so the store was firebombed and smoke began to filter into the Fillmore's auditorium. The Who were playing "Shakin' All Over" and the promoter Bill Graham was just about to come on and make an announcement, when Officer Daniel Mulhearn, a plain-clothes cop with the Tactical Police Force, leaped on stage and grabbed Daltrey's mike.

The Who had been touring for years now and reacted instinctively. Roadie Tony Haslam grabbed Officer Mulhearn from behind in a bear hug. Daltrey threw a punch, while Townshend aim a kick at the officer's groin. The battered cop only escaped the onslaught by jumping six feet from the stage. After the fracas, the 2,000-strong audience was evacuated safely and the second show was canceled.

But the police were not about to leave it at that. They headed to Loew's Midtown Hotel where the band were staying to arrest them. But The Who weren't there. They holed up that night at Bill Graham's apartment on East Seventh Street.

The band could not stay fugitives from justice for long,

though. The following day, May 17, *Tommy* was to be released in the U.S. and a boxed set of four singles—"Amazing Journey"/"Acid Queen," "Go To The Mirror"/"Tommy Can You Hear Me," "Smash The Mirror"/"Sensation," and "Sally Simpson"/"I'm Free"—along with an outline of the plot was being sent out to the radio stations. In addition, The Who were to appear again that night in the Fillmore East, with two more performances the following day. So Townshend and Daltrey voluntarily gave themselves up to the Ninth Precinct where they were formally charged with assaulting an officer in the performance of his duty. Given their violent behavior on stage, being arrested for assaulting an officer during a show can hardly be considered bad publicity. The album quickly climbed to number four in the U.S. and number two in the U.K.

Daltrey and Townshend were bailed until May 27, when the case was adjourned. On June 20, they finally appeared before the Supreme District Court in Manhattan. The charges against Daltrey were dropped, but Townshend was found guilty on the reduced charge of harassment and fined $75.

The Who played their two scheduled shows at the Fillmore on May 17. On May 18, they played three shows, adding an afternoon performance to make up for the second show that had been canceled on May 16.

On May 19, they appeared at the Rock Pile Club in Toronto, Canada. Then they moved on via the Capitol Theater in Ottawa and Electric Factory in Philadelphia, Pennsylvania, to the Merriweather Post Pavilion in Columbia, Maryland, where they were to play their one and only gig with Led Zeppelin. It was an experience they did not want to repeat.

"I had the unenviable task of throwing Zeppelin off the stage," said John "Wiggy" Wolff, who had been a roadie with the band since 1966 and had taken over day-to-day management of The Who from Chris Stamp and Kit Lambert in 1969. "They were playing over time, stringing it out, and there was a curfew, so I was saying, 'I've got to get you off!' I had to pull the plug on them, otherwise we were never going to go on."

Zeppelin plainly did not enjoy the experience either. They were to have appeared on the same bill as The Who again in St. Louis, Missouri, the following Sunday, but pulled out.

The Who went on to the Kinetic Playground in Chicago, Illinois, where they were supported by Joe Cocker and the Grease Band. Also on the bill, inexplicably, was the great jazz drummer Buddy Rich and his Orchestra. Moon stood spellbound in the wings watching him.

Then The Who took the stage and went into *Tommy*.

"Halfway through, all of a sudden, everybody realized that something was working," said Townshend. "I don't know quite what it was, but everybody all at the same time just stood up and stayed standing up. From that moment on they would always stand up at exactly the same point… It was the first time we had created a theatrical device that worked the same every time."

No one could really explain what was going on. The Who had somehow established an almost mystical communication with their audience. However, it became clear to Townshend that, when the band was singing "Listening to you…," the audience took this as, not a hymn to Meher Baba, but a homage to themselves. The Who, they believed, were listening to them.

By this time *Tommy*, which had been out for just two weeks in the U.S., had sold more than 200,000 copies, giving The Who their first gold record for selling more than $1,000,000-worth of discs in the U.S. This astonishing success was partly because of the band's tour. It was also helped by certain underground F.M. stations that, because of the band's controversial anti-establishment profile, played the double album back to back. In the U.K., though, where The Who were still thought of as a singles band only, sales were slower.

Hearing *Tommy* on record was one thing. In performance, the band had now raised the album to a new level. Inspired by seeing Buddy Rich, Keith Moon began playing the drums like the devil was driving him. The motionless Entwistle became a sinister brooding presence, wearing ever-more-outrageous suits. Pete Townshend, dressed in a boiler suit, put on a display of gymnastics, while long, curly-haired Roger Daltrey, dressed in a buckskin suit with a fringed jacket, had developed a new stage persona and seemed to transform himself into Tommy, experiencing everything the deaf, dumb, and blind boy went through.

For the next three weeks The Who continued touring across America. They had the same effect wherever they went.

At the Fillmore West in San Francisco, California, The Who were supposed to play two shows a night, supported by the Woody Herman Jazz Band. But they had to cancel the second show on June 19 to catch the 11.30 p.m. plane back to New York to make their court appearance the next morning. As it was, they had to leave the stage from the first show while the audience were still begging for an encore.

After the court hearing, The Who stayed on for another week in New York City. On their last night, they met with their U.S. agent Frank "the Tank" Barsalona of Premier Talent in his apartment on West 57th Street. Barsalona had ready booked Joe Cocker, Ten Years After, and other Premier acts to appear that Woodstock Music and Arts Fair that August. Townshend did not want to do it.

Woodstock had been billed as "three days of peace and music" and Pete was very anti the whole hippie movement that was manifesting itself in the U.S.

"I didn't at all like Haight-Ashbury," he said. "I didn't like fucking Abbie Hoffman [leader of the Yippie Party]. I didn't like Timothy Leary [the L.S.D. guru who said 'Turn on, tune in, drop out']. And I didn't like Woodstock."

But after a long night of negotiation with the band, John Wolff struck deal.

"Pete was really pissed off with the whole thing," said Wolff later. "He was outnumbered, and he was doing a bit of a number."

The band had already agreed to play the Tanglewood Music Festival outside Lenox, Massachusetts, which was being promoted by Bill Graham, on August 12—just week before Woodstock. Graham was giving them $12,500. But that would only cover their airfares, their gear, and other expenses. So for Woodstock, Wolff held out for the same amount.

Back in London, The Who were supposed to headline the final night of the "Pop Proms," a week-long series of concerts at the Royal Albert Hall, which were supposed to ape the classical Promenade Concerts—popularly known as the "Proms"—that are staged there every year. They were to appear with Chuck Berry and walked right into a dispute about billings. This was resolved when they agreed to support Chuck Berry in the first show, while he supported them in the second. This was not a good solution. The audience of the first house was crammed with Teddy Boys. As old fashioned rock and rollers, they had come to see Chuck Berry. Traditional enemies of the Mods, they had no time for the new arty stuff The Who had come up with in *Tommy*.

They tried to stop The Who coming onstage and trashed the seats—this was a traditional activity of the Teds since Bill Haley and the Comets had first toured the U.K. in February 1957. Sharpened coins were thrown. One cut Daltrey on the forehead. There was a running battle with the Albert Hall ushers and the police. One of The Who's roadies, Tony Haslam, had brought a mace gun back with him from the U.S. and fired it into the crowd. The response was a barrage of coins and cans.

The M.C., Jeff Dexter, who had been taking cover behind The Who's speakers, emerged and tried to calm the situation with the new hippie-speak of "peace and love." This did not go down at all well. Then he said, "Look, we all love rock and roll, we all love Chuck Berry, and The Who love Chuck Berry. The Who have done something new, now you've got to try and dig it."

By this time, the police had managed to get the hard-core trouble-makers out of the hall. The rest of the audience began to settle down. But they were not going to hear something new. *Tommy* might go down big with audiences in the U.S., but it was not going to work in the U.K. The Who placated the audience with old rock numbers such as "Shakin' All Over" and "Summertime Blues."

The second house was more appreciative, though. They were in a mellow mood having come directly from the Rolling Stones free concert in nearby Hyde Park. And they were the perfect audience for the U.K. premiere of *Tommy*.

Backstage at the Royal Albert Hall, after the "Pop Proms" on July 5, 1969, just a month and a half after *Tommy* was released, Townshend told *Melody Maker* that Universal International Pictures had made an offer for the screen rights. The group were to have a hand in the screenplay, but not in the direction of the movie.

"We'll be working with a scriptwriter," he said, "but at the moment we haven't really got anybody lined up at all. All we've got is the budget of a couple of million dollars."

On December 4, 1969, *Disc* magazine published a story saying that there were plans to turn *Tommy* into a cartoon movie. It was to be made up the animator George Dunning, who had made the Beatle's *Yellow Submarine* the year before.

"It will not just be a straight, narrative version of *Tommy*," the magazine reported, "but an extension of the album. Pete might write some new material for it, and the name might even be changed."

The magazine also reported that *Tommy* was being expanded and turned into a ballet—one rumor that did turn out to be true.

The Who went on to tour a variety of venues in England. It did no good. Tommy did not have the same electrifying effect on British audiences. U.K. sales had peaked the week before they appeared at the Albert Hall, while they were still riding high in the States, and *Tommy* had dropped out of the U.K. album charts altogether by the time they had reached the end of the U.K. tour at Plumpton racecourse on August 9. It made sense to go back to the U.S., where the single "I'm Free," with "We're Not Gonna Take It" on the B-side was in the charts.

"I'm Free," with "1921" on the B-side, did not chart in the U.K. Nor did a flurry of other singles from *Tommy*—"Go To The Mirror"/"Sally Simpson," "The Acid Queen"/"We're Not Gonna Take It," and "Christmas"/ "Overture"—released that July.

On August 12, The Who appeared as special guest stars supporting Jefferson Airplane at Tanglewood. Traditionally Tanglewood in west Massachusetts had been a classical music venue. This was the first time it had staged rock acts, but that crossover made it an ideal arena for *Tommy*. It was everything that Woodstock was not.

The legendary Woodstock Music and Arts Fair was held in upstate New York on August 15, 16, and 17, 1969. It was billed as "three days of peace and music." *Time* magazine called it "history's largest happening... one of the most significant political and social events of the age." It is estimated that as many as 400,000 people attended. Many more saw news coverage of the festival on T.V. Since then millions have seen Warner Brothers' movie of the festival. Although Woodstock had all the trappings of a hippie, counter-culture event, it was run by four young rock entrepreneurs who had pre-sold the movie and recording rights.

The festival had all the makings of a disaster. When they heard that a huge rock festival was being organized, the people of Woodstock complained that there town was too small and ill-equipped to handle it. The organizers retained the Woodstock name when they moved the proposed venue to Wallkill—which had second thoughts—then to White Lake in the town of Bethel, 60 miles from Woodstock, where it was eventually staged. The venue—Max Yasgur's 600-acre dairy farm—was only settled upon less than a month before the festival and this last minute relocation meant that many of the amenities the organizers had planned failed to materialize. The crowd was twice the size that anyone had expected. They jammed the roads for 20 miles around the site. Thousands of festival-goers abandoned their automobiles and walked the last few miles. Because there were no proper fences or gates, most of the crowd had to be let in free, causing financial problems for the organizers. The huge crowds made it difficult to bring in food and medicine and evacuate those who had fallen ill. The National Guard, the U.S. Army, and local community, business, and religious organizations arrived to lend a hand.

The ground was already muddy from three weeks of summer showers. The festival was repeatedly drenched with rain and the site turned into a quagmire—the New York *Daily News* called the festival "a morass of mud, music, and misery." Few of the visitors were equipped to camp out. Electricity supplies, fresh water, food, garbage collection, and sewerage systems were constantly on the verge of breaking down.

"It was a city dump," wrote the *New York Post*. "The flies clung to your arms. The stench attacked your stomach." Many of the revelers where drunk, stoned on marijuana, or tripping on L.S.D. One died and many others needed medical attention. "The police feared a major medical crisis because of the nightlong rain which created huge pools of mud," the *Post* added.

Although the big acts of the time—the Beatles, the Rolling Stones, Bob Dylan, and the Doors—were not there, fans got to seen Richie Havens, Janis Joplin, Jock Cocker, Jefferson Airplane, Creedence Clearwater Revival, the Band, and—of course—The Who. Crosby, Stills and Nash became Crosby, Stills, Nash and Young in a performance that seemed to symbolize the hippie ethos of the show. Country Joe and the Fish, who played their anti-Vietnam War song "I-Feel-Like-I'm-Fixin'-To-Die Rag," and Jimi Hendrix—whose electric-guitar version of "The Star-Spangled Banner" was the climax of the show—made Woodstock part rock concert, part anti-war demonstration. The hippies coped well with the conditions, playing in the mud and bathing naked in the nearby lake.

Those who attended it and young people everywhere hailed the festival as the founding of the "Woodstock nation." Hippies, it seemed, could organize things for themselves, outside "straight" society. But they did not see the bitter backstage wrangling that resulted in years of lawsuits. Even the older generation, at the time, thought that a new age—the age of Aquarius—might just be dawning.

Max Yasgur, the farmer who had hired out his fields for the festival, said, "If a half million young people at the Aquarian Festival could turn such adverse conditions—filled with the possibility of disaster, riot, looting, and catastrophe—into three days of music and peace, then perhaps there is hope, that if we join with them, we can turn those adversities that are the problems of America today into a hope for a brighter and more peaceful future."

Woodstock was a financial disaster for the organizers. Although they had received a $1,000,000 advance on the movie of *Woodstock*, they had secured only a tiny royalty. By the movie's re-release in 1979, it had already brought Warner Brothers a worldwide box office gross of $50,000,000. Around 80 lawsuits were filed against the festival and the organizers themselves fell out in a $10,000,000 court action. Far from being the dawning of a new age, in retrospect, Woodstock marked the end of it.

The Who were flown part-way to the festival by helicopter. They were supposed to have traveled the last leg of the journey by car, but the roads were jammed. Eventually they had to walk—the last mile through thick mud. By the time they arrived, the organization of the festival had practically collapsed. They faced a 14-hour wait backstage. Nor was the band's temper helped when they heard that the balance of their $12,500 performance fee was being withheld. Townshend was particularly scathing.

"Listen, this is the fucking American dream, it's not my dream," he ranted. "I don't want to spend the rest of my life in fucking mud, smoking fucking marijuana. If that's the American dream, let's have our fucking money and piss off back to Shepherd's Bush where people are people."

John Wolff tackled the organizers, telling them that the band would not wait any longer. He was told that he could have a check.

"I'm not interested in a check," said Wolff. "Where's the money?"

For the next few hours the organizers studiously avoided him. As the time approached when The Who were due on stage, he was told they would have to go on—they would not be able to let down such a huge crowd.

"I don't care," said Wolff. "They're not going on."

Eventually, the organizers had to get a helicopter to fetch a bank manager as the safe was time-locked and he was the only one who could open it. Wolff got the cash, only to find himself surrounded by other bands that had not been paid.

The Who were due to go on at 10 p.m. But Sly and the Family Stone, who were on before them, played for three hours, and the band before them had overrun too. The Who finally went on at four in the morning.

"It was a joke," said Wolff.

Townshend was not in the best of moods. After 14 hours sitting on a plank in the rain, his coffee had been spiked with acid just before he was about to go on.

"All these hippies were wandering around thinking that the world was going to be different from that day on," he said. "As a cynical English arsehole I walked through it all and felt like spitting on the lot of them and shaking them, trying to make them realize that nothing had changed and nothing was going to change. Not only that, what they thought was an alternative society was basically a field full of six-foot-deep mud laced with L.S.D. If that was the world they wanted to live in, then fuck the lot of them."

He cleared the stage of photographers, including the Warner Brothers' film crew under director Mike Wadleigh, whose cash was just about the only thing that was keeping the show going.

Daltrey said that Woodstock was one of The Who's worst shows. The band's tight, hard-edged style clashed with the mellow, drug-induced self-indulgence of the other bands appearing. They were completely out of place. Things were not made better when, halfway through *Tommy*, Abbie Hoffman—anti-Vietnam war activist and founder of the Youth International Party, the "Yippies"—came onstage to complain about the jailing of his fellow Yippie John Sinclair for the possession of marijuana.

"Fuck off my fucking stage," Townshend yelled at Hoffman, then whacked him with his guitar sending Hoffman crashing into the camera pit.

"It was the most political thing I ever did," said Townshend.

But The Who stole the show in spite of everything.

Just as they reached the climatic finale of "We're Not Gonna Take It" with the bare-chested Roger Daltrey going into "See Me Feel Me," the first rays of dawn came over the horizon, flooding the stage with sunlight. It was the most uncanny effect.

"God was our lighting man," said Entwistle.

"When the sun came up, I just didn't believe it," said Townshend. "It was just incredible. I really felt we didn't deserve it, in a way. We put out such bad vibes."

"See Me Feel Me" became the climax of the movie *Woodstock*—along with "My Generation" and "Summertime Blues." This brought The Who and *Tommy* to a huge new international audience. "We're Not Gonna Take It" also appeared on the *Woodstock* album, put out after the festival.

The movie premiered on March 26, 1970 in the Trans-Lux East Theater in New York and the Fox-Wilshire in Hollywood. And it opened in London at the Empire Cinema, Leicester Square on June 25. This gave the sales of *Tommy* a whole new lease of life. The $35 album stayed in the U.S.

charts for 126 weeks, breaking The Who as recording artists in America and, finally, paying for all that broken equipment.

After Woodstock, The Who went back on tour in an effort to promote the album, even though Townshend was heartily sick of it.

"We just kind of kept playing *Tommy*, and playing *Tommy*, and playing *Tommy*, and then reviving *Tommy*," he said. "And then just when *Tommy* was about to go to sleep and we were gonna get on to our next project, Woodstock came along and it went back to number one... It was another nine months of walking *Tommy* around, this time with Roger in his Woodstock incarnation... that was even tougher 'cause by then I was really fed up with *Tommy*; and extremely fed up with Roger's chest."

On Saturday, August 30, they headlined at the second Isle of Wight Festival, Britain's version of Woodstock. Although the reclusive Bob Dylan was going to make his first appearance in Britain the following day, The Who stole the show.

Having learned their lesson from Woodstock, they helicoptered right into the festival site. Unfortunately, as they landed a huge board, lifted into the air by the downdraft, collapsed and smashed into the helicopter.

"It was a total disaster," said the show's M.C. Jeff Dexter, "because The Who intended to leave straight after they'd finished playing."

But The Who were adamant and Track had to send another helicopter.

On stage, they had one of the biggest P.A.s available in the U.K. at the time. It was rated at over 2,500 watts and people were warned not to stand within 50 feet of the speakers. This time the U.K. audience was ready for *Tommy*. The Who were now on a roll.

"It was a great concert for us," said Townshend. Unlike at Woodstock, they felt completely in control of the situation. "We were able to just come in, do it, and not need to know anything about what was going on. In other words, we didn't spend time at the festival getting into the vibrations, didn't stay to see Bob Dylan, didn't care what was going on. We knew that the stage act we had, with *Tommy* in it, would work under any circumstances because it had worked so many times on tour."

Even so, the performance just seemed to get better and better. In a 1971 interview with *Zigzag* magazine, Townshend reckoned that that their show at the Fairfield Halls, Croydon, Surrey, on September 21, 1969 was perhaps the best performance of *Tommy*. But it was exhausting. Before *Tommy* The Who's standard set had last just over an hour. Now it ran to two-and-a-half hours.

The show began with a number of early hits and stage favorites, to get the audience warmed up. Then they launched into *Tommy*. Omitting only "Cousin Kevin," "Underture," and "Welcome"—all 18 minutes 44 seconds of them—they would play the other 56 minutes 14 seconds of *Tommy* without a break. They found that it did not matter if they left out songs, even if they carried some of the narrative weight. *Tommy* did not work just as a story, it was a piece of music that was held together by its emotional power.

After they had finished *Tommy*, they would go into "Summertime Blues" and "Shakin' All Over" to dispel the elevated air that the opera had created. Then they would finish with "My Generation" and a quick reprise of *Tommy*, which was still in the music stores—as if to top and tail their chart career. Sometimes, if they could muster the energy for an encore, they would play "Magic Bus."

Although the rock opera worked as a single piece on a large stage, later in their careers and in smaller venues The Who found that it worked just as well in an abridged or truncated form. They played numerous heavily edited versions to suit the line-up on stage. Even so, the effect is always the same.

"The finale of *Tommy* never failed mesmerize me and the audience," said Townshend of the stage version. "It always felt to me like a prayer. I always felt myself full of Meher Baba when we performed it."

And *Tommy* had changed The Who as a band on stage.

"*Tommy* was huge. It made Roger into a proper front man," Townshend realized some time later. "He was magnificent on stage from this time forward. I felt as if a huge weight had been lifted. I think I probably resented that there was yet another glamour boy on stage—apart from Keith and his goo-goo eyes—but the pros outweighed the cons. The women backstage were a lot prettier. And Roger was almost always very, very happy."

Tommy turned Daltrey a rock-and-roll icon like Jim Morrison of the Doors or Robert Plant of Led Zeppelin.

But Kit Lambert and Chris Stamp had one more masterstroke to perform. They booked *Tommy* into an opera house. On September 29, 1968 the rock opera took to the stage of the Concertgebouw in Amsterdam, the Netherlands, for what the opera house billed as its "world premiere."

Keith Moon was so eager to get on stage that, as they were coming down, the carpeted stairs onto the stage, he started running. He sped across the stage and fell of the edge, knocking down two speakers. The opera audience, unused to such antics, laughed. Moon emerged covered with blood. The opera was well received by the concert-hall audience and a recording of the show was broadcast on Dutch T.V. the following night. It was brilliant coup. For the first time a rock band had appeared in the hallowed home of high art. Lambert and Stamp then worked tirelessly to put The Who on stage in opera houses across West Germany, Denmark, and France, bringing rock music to a new audience, and *Tommy* became a well respected operatic work. Later The Who became the first rock group to play at New York's Metropolitan Opera House. With 4,000 seats, it was the biggest opera house in the world. This was something the Beatles and Bob Dylan had only dreamed of. Four Mods from Shepherd's Bush had moved pop music into the mainstream of classical music. They were playing venues that had heard nothing more recent than Wagner and were reviewed by critics who thought jazz was avant-garde—or, as Keith would put it, Ava Gardner.

After Amsterdam, The Who took *Tommy* on a second, month-long, tour of North America. When they turned up at the Fillmore East for six nights. John Entwistle sarcastically referred to this as a "residency" and said that the same people turned up the front row each night.

Despite the fact that The Who did not wait around to see Bob Dylan on the Isle of Wight, he turned up to see them at the Fillmore. Composer and conductor of the New York

Philharmonic Orchestra Leonard Bernstein came backstage with his daughter.

"He was incredibly excited," said Townshend.

Bernstein shook his hand and grabbed him by the shoulders. "Do you realize what you are doing?" he said. "Do you realize how wonderful this is?"

Since writing the score for *West Side Story*, which is based on Shakespeare's *Romeo and Juliet*, in 1957, Bernstein had become passionate about making classical art accessible to a popular audience.

Not that they did not have time off. In late October, Townshend took off to Florida with John Wolff. They stayed with Tom Wright on his father's farm, some 50 miles north of Clearwater. It was there that Townshend wrote "The Seeker."

He was drunk in the middle of a swamp and covered in the prickly burrs of the local sandspur grass, which stick to your skin. He kept falling over, making the pain excruciating. Then the line came to him "I'm looking for me, you're looking for you, we're looking at each other and we don't know what to do." "The Seeker" was to be their first post-*Tommy* single.

Townshend was also moving in a new direction in an effort to put *Tommy* behind him. On October 27, his title music for a documentary film about the work of CERN—the European Council for Nuclear Research—who operate a huge subatomic particle accelerator under the Franco-Swiss border, aired on the B.B.C.

Returning to England in mid-November, The Who completed their U.K. *Tommy* tour. The biggest concert of the tour was on December 14 in the Coliseum in London's West

End—home of the English National Opera. Introducing *Tommy* on stage, Townshend drew a laugh and threw down a challenge.

"I'm a bit embarrassed to use the term 'opera' here in the Coliseum," he said. "I went to Covent Garden [the Royal Opera House] last night... Not bad, but not as good as us. Now we're going to take over."

Again the gig was filmed, but the poor lighting made the footage too poor to use at the time. However, "I'm Free" from the Coliseum concert appeared on the video compilation *Who's Better, Who's Best*, which was released in the U.K. in March, 1988 and in the U.S. in November of the same year.

opera-ting Tommy

By 1970, *Tommy* was fast becoming bigger than The Who. It was to become an albatross around their necks. Old pre-*Tommy* fans thought *Tommy* was a betrayal of rock and roll, and they looked down on new post-*Tommy* fans. This broke The Who's audience into two. And the old rock-and-rollers had a point. With *Tommy* appearing in opera houses, rock and roll was going legit.

Townshend said that when they got on a plane to fly to a gig, the air hostess would say to them, "I know who you are—you're Tommy the Who."

According to Townshend, this happened lots of times. Townshend said that he also saw posters saying, *"Tommy* and The Who." The deaf, dumb, and blind kid was getting top billing over the band.

In February 1970 they released "The Seeker" in the U.K., and in April in the U.S. It was another hymn to Meher Baba—although Townshend denied any specific connection.

"It was a song glorifying the ordinary man in the street, who's like hitting people with bottles but still, believe it or not, looking for god realization, even though he doesn't know it," he said.

Despite his protests, his demo of "The Seeker" appeared on an album called *Happy Birthday* made for Townshend's 26th birthday. Only 2,500 copies of this limited edition L.P. were pressed and they were only available—with a 28-page booklet containing poems and drawings inspired by Meher

Baba—from the Universal Spiritual League in London and the Meher Baba Information Office in Berkeley, California. All profits went to the Meher Baba Foundation, naturally.

For all its virtues, "The Seeker" was not a track from *Tommy*. It stalled at number 44 in the U.S. and number 19 in the U.K. As Roger Daltrey had predicted, The Who truly were an album band now. And, like it or not, they were now seen as head of the new progressive rock movement that was starting in Britain with Pink Floyd, Genesis, Yes, King Crimson, and Van Der Graaf Generator. The band members were not happy about this.

"All that guitar smashing and stuff went out of the window," said Entwistle. "We turned into snob rock. We were the kind of band Jackie Onassis would come and see, and I didn't particularly like that. I felt we should have played opera houses and smashed them up."

Townshend was not happy either and complained that they were now playing venues where only one per cent of the kids who wanted to see them could get in.

"The first 20 rows would be Polydor people," he said. "or Prince Rainier and his royal family, and honestly it was such a bad scene."

The Who struck back with *Live At Leeds*, which was recorded on February 14, 1970 during the Tommy tour. It was released in May in the U.K. and the U.S. in May. *Live At Leeds* was the antithesis of the studio albums the other progressive rock bands were making. And they had not even chosen a particularly prestigious venue to record in. The album was recorded at Leeds University in Yorkshire, 170 miles north of London.

"I'd been planning a live album for ages," said Townshend. "We recorded all the shows on the last American tour thinking that would be where we would get the best material. When we got back, we had 80 hours of tape, and, well, we couldn't sort that lot out, so we booked the Pye mobile studio and took it to Leeds. It turned out to be one of the best and most enjoyable gigs we've ever done."

Townshend was modest at best about the results.

"People always talk about The Who being good on stage," he said. "We're all about visual pop flash and in the past when we've recorded shows the tapes have sounded very grotty at best. When I should have been playing the guitar I'd have been waving my arms about like a windmill or when Keith should have been playing he's have been yelling 'ooh-ya-ooh-ya' at the top of his voice like Lennie Hastings. So what I want to do is sophisticate the sound a little. One trouble is Moon—he's so deafening. If we do a two-and-a-half hour show he just starts playing like a machine. I sure he puts out more watts than the rest of us put together."

In *The New York Times*, Nik Cohn gave it high praise. He said, "*Tommy* is rock's first formal masterpiece. *Live At Leeds* is the definitive hard-rock holocaust. It is the best live rock album ever made," in his column. It went to number four in the U.S. and three in the U.K.

All the press adulation worried Townshend.

Tommy, he said, "was highly overrated because it was rated where it shouldn't have been and it wasn't rated where it should have been." In his view, "It should have been rated as a successful attempt to tell a story in rock music. I don't listen to it…"

As a group, The Who joked about *Tommy* being a true opera—"which it isn't," said Townshend, "but The Who's audience and many of the rock press took it very seriously. It was this seriousness that ultimately turned *Tommy* into light entertainment."

But this did not belie how much he had enjoyed making it. "We were going down the drain. We needed challenging after putting out corny singles like 'Magic Bus' and 'Dogs.' Making *Tommy* really united us as a group and that was the good thing about it. The problem is that it has elevated The Who to heights they haven't attained."

The problem for Townshend was that he no longer liked the album now that they had done it live.

"We perform it much better on stage," he said, "and it's very hard to like the album after you've done it on stage. It was a real turn-on before we did it on stage."

Townshend also said that he was grateful that he had the other members of The Who to write for.

"I set myself a problem with *Tommy*, something to get down to," he said. "The Who will always respond to a challenge. A group like us always needs as much prestige as it can get and at the moment that's rock opera. On the Continent, *Tommy* was very successful and it brought a lot of kids who hadn't seen us."

Townshend conceded *Tommy* was not to everyone's taste.

"I can understand people not liking *Tommy* at all," he said. But he had a word for the critics in the press, "One of the basic problems of pop is that there are too many analysts. They should either like it or not, if it does something to them or not. They don't have to go into it."

Townshend was particularly critical of the level of analysis *Tommy* was getting in the U.S.

"*Tommy* was written with the idea that it would musically bridge the gap between The Who on stage and The Who on record—a gap that was getting wider by the moment," he told Penny Valentine from the U.K.'s *Disc and Music Echo*. "In the end *Tommy* swept away both sides of the argument. It got rid of the aggressive guitar bashing non-musical Who and the recording studio Who. That album earned us a whole new batch of fans— a lot of them quite honestly, I would be pleased to lose again. Especially the American pseudo-intellectuals who kept reading things into it. I would have thought that was impossible—for God's sake, it was a story and very clear at that."

Meanwhile, The Who toured the U.S. again—starting with two performances at the Met. on June 7, 1970. They had to pay the Met.'s union stagehands twice the normal rate as they were bringing their own equipment and they had to take out extra insurance in case the crowd was rowdy. But the Met. were pleased to see them.

"All productions of quality come to the Met.," said assistant manager Herman Krawitz. Justifying *Tommy's* appearance at the world's largest opera house, he said, "It's a story with music and words… It uses the methods and means of opera. It's opera in a new language. Is it an opera that we'll have in our repertory? I don't know. Not right away. Perhaps in the future."

Fans queued over the weekend to get tickets. These were available only from the Fillmore as a gesture to The Who's rock fans. They sold out completely in just eight hours, grossing $55,000.

This time, The Who aimed to shake opera lovers up. They flew in three tons of equipment, including a 4,000-watt stereo P.A., designed by Townshend and Who soundman Bob Pridden.

"We hit them head on," said Moon. "It was the first time a group had played at the Met.—and probably the last." He was right about that.

He regretted that he had not been able to rig up any explosions to occur during the show—"although we had the usual ending—a riot. Nothing too serious, just clapping and stamping."

Some 8,000 people turned out for the two shows. Bejeaned rock fans mixed with the tuxedoed and evening-gowned opera crowd. Despite the forebodings of some opera-goers, one usher said, "These kids are much more polite than their parents.

The New York Times devoted a whole page to the event, saying, "For five hours yesterday the Metropolitan Opera House became the Fillmore North."

The *Times'* opera critic attempted to rationalize *Tommy's* appeal to the young. "Many young people today firmly believe they have been traumatized into something figuratively akin to autism, and it has left them functionally blind, deaf and dumb to the values of the gerontocracy that rules them and us all. So they are evolving what they hope are their own 'miracle cures,' among which pop music is one of the more potent."

It should be remembered that all these events were occurring at a time when America was terribly split between the young, who protested against the war in Vietnam as their generation was having to fight it, and the older generation, who retained the values of duty, patriotism, and self-sacrifice that had seen the U.S. through World War II.

The Who's appearance at the Met. even made the evening news with C.B.S. broadcasting backstage interviews and footage from the early show. Kit Lambert was beside himself with excitement.

"I timed the calls for encores," said Brian Somerville, a spokesman for the group. "At the first concert the applause lasted 11 minutes and at the evening shows, 14 minutes. Rudolph Bing, who runs the opera house, said he said seen nothing like it since before the war in the days of grand opera."

Tommy at the Met. did end with a Who moment, though. After the second show, 300 fans besieged the stage, demanding an encore. But the band members were exhausted and Townshend returned to the stage to make his apologies.

"Thank you," he said. "We'd do more, but we're really tired after two shows of two hours each."

Some people booed.

"After two fucking hours, boo to you, too," he yelled.

Then he lobbed the microphone into the audience and stormed off stage. Despite this, Townshend was pleased that they had performed at the Met.

"It was an affirmation not only that rock had to be take seriously but of our very existence as human beings," he said. "It seemed to me to be a very mature and sensible gesture that we and our fans should be invited to a place like the Met. It's a wonderful notion, the idea of a snotty pop group playing opera houses. But we actually did it... We shat in their toilet!"

But some of the snootier critics remained dismissive. Rock-and-roll purist Al Aronowitz wrote in *Rolling Stone*, "*Tommy* is the story of a boy who becomes deaf, dumb, and blind after witnessing the murder of his mother's lover by his natural father, who has just returned from among the missing at the close of World War I. Before he is cured to become a religious leader, Tommy gets molested by a perverted uncle and is slipped some L.S.D. by an unscrupulous gypsy. We learn all this from the program. Otherwise the whole thing may as well be sung in Italian."

However, *The New York Times* concluded their review with, "Awake, the forces of the future are no longer standing at the gates. They are inside."

Lambert and Stamp tried to get *Tommy* on in Moscow directly after the performance at the Met. so that they could get the headline, "Rock Breaks The Iron Curtain." They petitioned the Soviet Embassy. Eventually they were offered a gig in the opera house in Leningrad—now St Petersburg. But the offer came too late.

The Met. show would be the last outing for the whole of *Tommy*, Townshend told the *New Musical Express*, although they would continue to perform the truncated version in their stage show. "It's becoming a bit of a monkey," he said, "like the breaking of the gear, people expect it."

Unfortunately—from the band's point of view at least—they could not abandon *Tommy* altogether.

"We're trying to get off it, although we've said that before," Keith Moon told *Melody Maker*. "But when we get down to rehearsing without doing *Tommy*, we have two numbers left."

When they reached Chicago on the 1970 tour, Townshend was forced to announce, "Something we've done 40 or more times and swore never to perform on the stage again."

There was a huge roar. The audience's reaction was so noisy that the band could not begin until Keith Moon got up and said, "It's a bloody opera. So sit down and shut up."

The *Chicago Tribune* said, "I'll bet there wasn't a person in the Auditorium Theater last night who won't tell you that this was probably the best concert Chicago has ever had. Even those who have seen Janis and Cocker and BS&T [Blood, Sweat, and Tears]. In *Tommy* alone there were five, six, seven, maybe eight standing ovations."

The Who's massive new P.A. had to be transported around the U.S. in a custom-built truck and they needed a five-man road crew to handle the equipment. This was the beginning of the great age of stadium tours. The Who were billed as "The Greatest Rock And Roll Band In The World"—a mantle later assumed by the Rolling Stones.

"We became an extraordinary machine," said Townshend. "There was no question about it. I used to wake up on the stage again every night and think: 'Oh my God, I'm riding this horse again.'"

The *Maryland Democrat* called seeing *Tommy* on stage, "Unbelievable! Remarkable! Outstanding! Or anything else you want to call better than the best."

The *San Francisco Chronicle* said it "was absolutely staggering in its emotional and musical power... writing about their music is something of an exercise in futility. It need not be explained to those who were there, it cannot be explained to those that were not. If a singe word can sum it up, that word is 'shattering.'"

And the *San Francisco Examiner* said that the audience, "had just heard the finest two hours of contemporary music of their lives. They knew it. The Who knew it... Exaggeration? I cannot exaggerate perfection."

On June 24, 1970, at the Spectrum Theater in Philadelphia, Pennsylvania, The Who were presented with plaques celebrating $5,000,000-worth of sales of *Tommy*. And it would go on selling. *Tommy* was released as a series of singles and, in the U.K., the double album and the two halves were sold separately as *Tommy Part 1* and *Tommy Part 2* in an effort to make it affordable to everyone.

But owning *Tommy* on vinyl and seeing The Who perform *Tommy* on stage were not enough sate the audience's appetite. The public wanted more. In April, an underground newspaper produced in Washington University in St. Louis, Missouri, printed the lyrics of what they called "an original rock opera: *Chancellor Tommy*." It was supposed to be a satire on campus politics, sung to the music of The Who's *Tommy*. However, the storyline was identical to *Tommy's* and most of the lyrics printed in the paper were a direct lift from Townshend's libretto.

Then on October 16—18, 1970, the unthinkable happened. *Tommy* became a ballet. Les Grands Ballets Canadiens put on a multi-media dance adaptation in Montreal, Canada. The following March there was another production as part of a college thesis at the University of South California. *Tommy* had gone intellectual.

Decca had been taken over by M.C.A./Universal Pictures, who now exercized their option on the screen rights and prepared to bankroll the shoot, with M.G.M. or Warner

Brothers handling the distribution. But Universal did not seem to know which way they wanted to go. Ray Stark, fresh from Barbra Streisand's *Funny Girl* (1968), was slated as producer, while Universal's chosen director was Joseph Strick, who directed heavyweight literature adaptations such as Jean Genet's *The Balcony* in 1963 and James Joyce's mammoth *Ulysses* in 1967.

Kit Lambert was working on the shooting script, but Townshend had already spent two years on the project and was sick of it. The two fell out.

"I was *Tommy* that destroyed the relationship," said Townshend after the split. "It was so exhausting... incredibly long and drawn out."

Universal eventually rejected Lambert's script and dropped the project when the band lost interest. The Who were now making up to $15,000 a concert, although they liked to stay in touch with the promoters and fans who had supported them on the way up and played smaller venues for half that amount. Sales of the album *Tommy* brought in $5,000,000 in the U.S. alone, with *Lives At Leeds* contributing another $1,000,000. Lambert and Chris Stamp now set about renegotiating The Who's contract. They signed an eight-album deal with M.C.A. for an advance amounting to $6,000,000.

Before *Tommy* The Who had been on the brink of bankruptcy. Now the individual members were millionaires. Roger Daltrey bought a six-bedroom Jacobean mansion built in 1620 in the small village of Burwash, East Sussex, southeast of London, and said that he never wanted to live in London again. He bought a herd of cows, took over two neighboring farms, and dug his own trout pond to that he could indulge in his life-long passion for fishing.

Pete Townshend gave a lot of his money to charity. John Entwistle used his to finance his own album *Smash Your Head Against The Wall* using songs he had written that he did not think were suitable for The Who, while Keith Moon simply pissed his money up the wall. He got drunk a lot and regularly turned up in costume. He would walk around the streets in a gorilla suit or dressed as a vicar. With Vivian Stanshall, he was ejected from a German *Bierkeller* in London's Mayfair district. They were dressed as Nazi leaders Adolf Hitler and Heinrich Himmler. After yelling *"Sieg heil"* they were escorted to the door by a large Teuton in *lederhosen*. A few hours later, they were seen, similarly attired, being chased around the North London Jewish suburb of Golders Green by a kosher butcher waving a meat cleaver.

Although many of his antics were amusing, there were concerns about Moon's mental health after a fracas with some skinheads which ended with Moon accidentally running over his 24-year-old driver Neil Boland with his Bentley. A wheel had gone over Boland's head, which cracked like an egg, and when Moon tried to extricate the body Boland's brains spilt out. Racked with guilt, Moon called himself a "murderous fuck." A verdict of accidental death was returned by the inquest, but Moon pleaded guilty to charges of drunken driving and driving without a license or insurance. The court accepted that Moon had not intended to drive—that's why had had a chauffeur with him—and had done so only to escape being set upon by the skinhead gang. He was given an absolute discharge.

The Who had other problems. Creatively, they had no idea where to go next. They talked of recording another double album, this time producing one side each. Townshend dabbled in journalism and film, then began thinking about writing another rock opera. This time he outlined the plot of his new *Tommy* to the British music magazine, *Disc and Music Echo*.

"It's about a set of musicians, a group who look and behave remarkably like The Who, and they have an idealized roadie, Bobby," said Townshend. "Anyway, this guy finds a musical note which basically creates complete devastation. And when everything is destroyed, only the real note, the true note that they have been looking for, is left."

But soon after, when asked what The Who planned to do next, Townshend told *New Musical Express*, "I dunno, really. Maybe we'll do a five album opera on a torso called *Deborah*."

In fact, in October 1971, The Who released the retrospective *Meaty Beaty Big and Bouncy*, which Townshend said was "probably the best ever Who album" though it contained no new material. By this time Townshend had written some new songs and they tried to drop *Tommy* from the act, but their fans continued to demand that they play it.

The ballet version went on tour in North America and finally arrived on Broadway where it ran for two weeks. Meanwhile a theatrical version debuted in Seattle and ran for three weeks. A production of *Tommy* ran for a month at the Aquarius Theater in Hollywood, California. This had Townshend's endorsement as it had earlier been presented at the University of Southern California in March 1971 to critical acclaim. But Track Records refused Lone Mountain College in San Francisco permission to take their production of *Tommy* on the road after 125 performances, because Track were trying to place the rights with a professional theater company. Then the New Seekers—a U.K./Australian clean-living close-harmony group more famous for "I'd Like To Teach The World To Sing (In Perfect Harmony)" which was adapted from Coca Cola ad—produced a medley of "Pinball Wizard" and "See Me Feel Me," which went to number 16 in the U.K. and number 29 in the U.S.

All this was becoming increasingly problematic for The Who. It seemed that they could not get out from under *Tommy* and they even considered splitting up. Eventually Townshend gave his permission for American producer Lou Reizner, who had produced albums for Rod Stewart in 1969 and 1970, to record an all-star version of *Tommy*. His hope was that, if there was another version that they could not be expected to perform on stage, they would be released from that obligation. For once, the band became enthusiastically involved the project. Lou Reizner "symphonized" Tommy, arranging it for a full symphony orchestra, using traditional classical techniques. It was to be performed by the 100-piece London Symphony Orchestra and the English Chamber Choir.

Reizner wanted Rod Stewart to play the character Tommy, but after some strong-arm work by Townshend, the role went to Daltrey. Instead Rod Stewart got to sing "Pinball Wizard." Steve Winwood—of the Spencer Davis Group, Powerhouse, Traffic, Blind Faith and Ginger Baker's Air Force—played Tommy's father. Maggie Bell of Stone the Crows was Tommy's mother. Graham Bell of the Chosen Few played her lover. African-American backing singer Merry Clayton played the Acid Queen. Sandy Denny of Fairport

Convention played the nurse. Richie Havens was the Hawker. Former Beatle Ringo Starr played Uncle Ernie. John Entwistle was Cousin Kevin and the actor Richard Harris played the doctor. The album took a year in the planning and eight months in the studio, costing £65,000 ($100,000). Townshend and Daltrey turned up to most of the recording sessions and Townshend provided acoustic guitar parts and vocals. Townshend also wrote "Love Reign O'er Me" for Maggie Bell. The track did not make the album, but appeared later on *Quadrophenia*.

Lou Reizner's *Tommy* was released in the U.K. in October 1972 and in the U.S. in November as a boxed set with a 28-page booklet. It went to number eight in the U.K. and number five in the U.S., where it went gold in a week. It sold 400,000 copies and stayed in the album charts in the U.S. for 38 weeks. Worldwide it sold over a million copies in less than four months. The *New Musical Express* called the album a "milestone on contemporary music" and the "best concept album every made," while *Melody Maker* said, "Townshend's masterpiece has finally got the treatment it deserves with an all-star cast, a full symphony orchestra and presentation that ranks among the best in the history of rock music." France's Académie du Disque awarded it its *grand prix*. A number of singles were issued off the back of the album on both sides of the Atlantic and Daltrey's version of "I'm Free" from the album reached number 13 in the U.K. singles chart. Now, at last, they could drop *Tommy* from their stage act.

"I don't think people will expect us to perform it," he told the *New Musical Express*. "But I think it will undoubtedly widen our audience, and we may pull in a few fans who wouldn't normally listen to the group."

Originally Townshend loved Reizner's recording. For him, it was as if the concept he originally had for *Rael* had been brought to life. Later he went off it. After being involved in some live performances of the symphonic version, he began to find it "bleak," even though he admitted it had more to it than the band's original recording.

In December 1972, Reizner's version of *Tommy* took to the stage for two sell-out shows at the Rainbow theater in Finsbury Park, North London, with Keith Moon taking over from Ringo Starr as Uncle Ernie and Peter Sellers replacing Richard Harris was the doctor. Daltrey even dusted off his old fringed 1969 stage costume for the occasion.

The producer, Don Hawkin, planned to turn the Rainbow into a huge pinball machine with the audience sitting in the playing area. But the Greater London Council refused permission for the alterations. Instead the pinball machine was confined to the stage with lights to ape the movement of the pinball. Other lighting effects were projected onto a huge screen above the stage. The production cost £12,000 ($18,000) to stage. It made almost £20,000 ($30,000) which was donated to the charity Stars Organization for Spastics.

Pete Townshend appeared as the narrator. He was a little drunk, visibly nervous, and missed several cues. In typical Townshend fashion, he abused the audience and pretended to wipe his ass with the script. Afterwards, he was a bit ashamed of his performance. He said he regretted taking part and donated his takings to a charity dedicated to providing music therapy for children.

As Townshend was not playing in the production, he could, for the first time, watch Daltrey's performance as if he was an ordinary member of the audience and was awestruck with it.

"He was great," said Townshend. "I'd always thought Roger was a bit naff. I'd always thought he was a bit of a nuisance—you know, swinging his microphone and getting in the way of the guitar sound. That was the moment I realized that, through *Tommy*, Roger had made his connection to the audience and become a theatrical performer. I had much greater respect for him after that."

In a triumphant climax to the show, Daltrey led the whole audience in singing "Listening To You." Afterwards he told *Record Mirror* how much he had missed playing the role of Tommy on stage.

"A lot of The Who has been lost in volume since we left *Tommy* out of the live show," he said. "It's lost some of the light and shade, and I've found it a lot less rewarding."

For Roy Carr of the *New Musical Express*, it was Keith Moon who stole the show. His Uncle Ernie, said Carr, was the "epitome of warped depravity to the extent you could all but smell him."

The Reizner version of *Tommy* was to have been staged again at the Royal Albert Hall in London, with profits going to charity, but it was canceled when the Hall's management objected to the content of the opera.

"The manager of the Albert Hall told me that he considered *Tommy* to be unsavory and that, in his estimation, it isn't an opera," said Reizner. "I am amazed that he is able to set himself up in judgment in this way."

Shows scheduled at New York's Radio City Music Hall, Nassau Coliseum, and the L.A. Forum were canceled, although an Australian production went ahead. Daltrey turned down the starring role, recalling how The Who had been received down under in 1968. But Keith Moon went.

"I went over there and just generally intimidated the Australian cast," said Moon. "Graham Bell came over with me. It was a good idea really because, with the experience we'd got from the London show, we were able to help the others because we'd seen how it worked in London."

Lou Reizner was also in Australia. The production there drew an audience of 30,000 to the outdoor Myer Music Bowl in Melbourne, Victoria. A second show at a racecourse in Sydney, New South Wales, was filmed and aired by Channel Seven. It won an Australian T.V. award for being the year's most outstanding creative production.

Another production was staged in London on December 13 the following year. This featured David Essex as the narrator, Roy Wood of The Move—and later Wizzard—in Rod Stewart's part, Marsha Hunt as the nurse, Elkie Brooks as Tommy's mother, Steve Marriott of the Small Faces as his father, and Vivian Stanshall as Uncle Ernie.

Once again Townshend praised the production, believing that the band was now free of *Tommy*.

"Naturally we're excited about new activity around the group," he told the *New Musical Express*, "but *Tommy* is now his own master. Anyway, we're now working on Jimmy."

Jimmy was the hero of Townshend's next project *Quadrophenia*. In it, Townshend tried to tell a more down-to-earth story. However, it lacked the clear narrative of *Tommy*.

Daltrey felt it needed too much explanation to get from one track to another and, although it went to number two on both sides of the Atlantic, the band thought of it as a failure. Meanwhile *Tommy* refused to lie down and die.

filming **Tommy**

There had been talk of turning *Tommy* into a movie from the beginning. Because Decca, The Who's record company in the U.S., had been taken over my M.C.A., the movie rights had gone to Universal, who were part of the group. Kit Lambert had written a script that Universal sat on for two years before rejecting it. They then refused to pay for the filming of *Tommy*.

Townshend found all this incredibly frustrating and blamed Lambert when the movie project foundered.

"Out relationship never really recovered," he said.

The idea of making a movie out of *Tommy* had not gone entirely cold, though. Woodstock and the Reizner revamp had kept *Tommy* in the public eye. Robert Stigwood, whose Creation label had helped The Who out when they were in dispute with Shel Talmy, expressed an interest. He had recently produced the movie version of *Jesus Christ, Superstar,* which was released in 1973.

The director Ken Russell, the bad boy of British cinema, was approached. He had cut his teeth making T.V. arts programs for the B.B.C. Then he made two feature films *French Dressing* in 1963 and *Billion Dollar Brain* in 1967. But it was *Women in Love,* based on the D.H. Lawrence novel, in 1969 that established his reputation as a bankable director. The visual beauty of this film and its tasteful handling of erotic scenes won the approval of both the critics and the box office. His next movie, *The Music Lovers* in 1970, portrayed the anguished life of the Russian composer Peter Ilyich Tchaikovsky. This was very much the sort of thing that he had done at the B.B.C., But the flamboyant, sensationalist style of the movie infuriated audiences.

His next movie, *The Devils*, which came out in 1971 and was based on the Aldous Huxley novel *The Devils of Loudon*, aroused even more controversy with its portrayal of mass sexual hysteria in a convent. Russell followed that with a camp version of the Sandy Wilson's 1920s style musical, *The Boy Friend* in 1971, *Savage Messiah* in 1972 which told the life story of the sculptor Henri Gaudier-Brzeska, who died in the trenches during World War I at the age of 23, and *Mahler*, starring Robert Powell, in 1974.

A classical music fan, Ken Russell said he preferred Lou Reizner's symphonic version of *Tommy* to The Who's original, but Townshend thought that Russell eventually came around and ended up preferring their version. Townshend prided himself that *Tommy* could break genres and reach out to an audience beyond traditional rock fans.

Despite Russell's initial misgivings, Townshend and Chris Stamp became convinced that he was the man for the job. But when they first went to visit Russell, they found that he lived up to his cantankerous reputation. Instead of discussing the film, Russell ranted about a movie project about Rabelaisian monks that he had just had to abandon. He outlined a plot that even bad boy of rock and roll Pete Townshend described as "hairy" and they began to get cold feet.

Sometime later, though, Townshend was out in London recording street sounds for the *Quadrophenia* album. He had the microphones hidden in a travel bag and the tape recorder in a suitcase. He wanted to record a little casual conversation to use as a sound effect and when he saw a bunch of men chatting he sidled up to them. But he was concentrating so hard on the recording, he did not notice who they were.

They turned out to be Russell, Stamp, and producer Mike Carreras. They were delighted to see him. They were about to have a meeting about the movie project and wanted Townshend there, and had been disappointed so far that day because they could not get hold of him.

Townshend was a great believer in coincidences. He believed that they revealed that higher forces were at work. From that moment, he knew the movie had to be made.

Unfortunately Russell was busy with another project at the time, so Townshend and Stamp began hunting round for another director.

"They would insist on buying me long drawn-out lunches 'to find out where your head is at,'" he complained, "and to ask me how I felt about it because they wanted to 'fit in with your ideas and conception.' In the end I thought if they wanted me to come up with the ideas then they could give me the money and I'd make it."

Eventually, as Stigwood got the money together, he managed to persuade Russell to join the project. This found favor all around. Once Townshend got to work closely with Ken Russell, he found him to be a deeply spiritual man who was fascinated by the mystical underpinnings of the story. But Russell also was a practical film-maker.

His philosophy of movie-making, he said, was "to entertain first, and the preaching comes second. Most of my films are based on that premise."

First he needed to make the narrative work in concrete, everyday terms, he said. Townshend himself had tried to do that while writing and recording the album. But he was only too conscious that, at some points, he had failed. The story was often disjointed and needed quite a bit of explaining. One problem occurs where Tommy's father, after his long absence, returns, and kills his wife's lover. On the album there was no lyric or musical effect that indicates the actually moment of death. This was key, because the whole story sprang from that one incident.

On the album Tommy's parents immediately launch into, "You didn't hear it, you didn't see it."

Townshend conceded that the listener could be forgiven if they asked, "Didn't hear and see what?"

Russell saw the problem immediately and completely altered the plot. Instead of the father killing Tommy's mother's lover, the lover would kill the father as this was surely a more traumatic event for a child. Tommy's dead father then became the focus of his spiritual quest. He becomes the mystical "master"—a figure Townshend had written about in his original notes.

It has to be said, that this switch did not completely solve the problem. After seeing the movie, people would ask, "What did they do with the body?"

But that would have been a problem either way around. Besides, by that point, Tommy was deaf, dumb, and blind, so even if the viewer did not see how the body was disposed of, any movie-goer who empathized with Tommy would not expect to.

To make *Tommy* a viable project financially, Stigwood needed stars. He brought in Ann-Margret, who had been nominated for an Oscar for *Carnal Knowledge* in 1971, and Jack Nicholson, who had shot to fame with *Easy Rider* in 1969, starred alongside Ann-Margret in *Carnal Knowledge*, had a hit that year with *Chinatown* in 1974, and would win an Oscar of Best Actor for *One Flew Over the Cuckoo's Next* in 1975, the year the movie of *Tommy* came out. Russell delivered Oliver Reed, his favorite actor, who he had already worked with in *Women In Love* and *The Devils*.

This caused problems for Townshend. When Stigwood phoned up to say he had just signed Jack Nicholson, Townshend said, "Who's Jack Nicholson?"

Stigwood said that he was one of the biggest stars in the U.S. at the time.

"Can he sing?" asked Townshend.

Stigwood said, "No."

"I'm not having another fucker in this film who can't sing," objected Townshend. "Oliver Reed is giving me nightmares as it is."

As it turned out, it was found that after a little practice, Reed could sing acceptably and his acting style fitted into the movie perfectly.

Russell wrote the screenplay. It was decided early on there should be no dialog. The story would be carried by the music. This would make the movie as true as possible to the album. However, it also meant that Townshend would have to write four new songs to fill in missing parts of the narrative and some of the existing material would have to be reworked to clarify the plotline. They would have to fit with Russell's timings for each scene and explain what was happening much more clearly than in the original. They would also have to be flexible in case things changed during shooting. So Townshend went back to work in The Who's Rampart Studios—an old church hall in Battersea, south London, that the band had converted into a state-of-the-art recording studio and rehearsal room in 1973.

The Who laid down the backing tracks that the actors were going to sing over. Elton John was called in to record "Pinball Wizard" and brought his stage band with him. Graham Deakin of Ox, the group of musicians who played on Entwistle's solo work, also turned up at the studios along with Mike Ralphs of Bad Company, Kenny Jones and Ron Wood from the Faces, Eric Clapton, session-man Nicky Hopkins who played piano, drummer Mike Kelly, guitarist Alan Ross who played with Entwistle's band, Ro Ro, backing singers Vicki Brown and Margo Newman who played the nurses in "It's A Boy," bassist Philip Chen of the Streetwalkers, Paul Gurvitz, drummer Tony Newman, singer Liza Strike, guitarist Caleb Quaye, bassist and vocalist Fuzzy Samuels who played on Stephen Stills' albums in the 1970s, Mylon LeFevre, and Joe Cocker's keyboard player Chris Stainton.

Jess Roden, leader singer of the Alan Bown Set who had provided backing vocals on "Magic Bus," was called in to lend a soulful, wailing voice behind Daltrey singing "Listening To You." Singer-songwriter Billy Nicholls and Townshend also provided backing vocals. They worked on them continuously for three weeks, trying to tailor everything to specific sections of Ken Russell's script. And Russell himself turned up in the studio more often than not.

Nicholls was surprised by Russell, who did not turn out to be the egotistic martinet he had imagined. Townshend had to put away his ego for the duration too. When Russell heard one piece that Townshend had composed on the synthesizer, he shook his head and said that he would not be able to match it visually.

"Towards the end of the sessions he seemed to get a little bit crazy," said Nicholls of the director. "As the music was getting finished he would be walking around the studio with a stick in his hand, beating out rhythms, getting more excited, suggesting more ideas, maybe getting a bit more pissed than he would have done earlier on. You could see he was beginning to feel things happening, beginning to see what he'd be doing with the music."

Daltrey was full of praise for Russell's contribution.

"I don't think anybody could do it except Ken Russell," he said. "We need a guy who we can relate to, feed information in to him, and get something back. Ken's the first bloke that's done that since our manager Kit Lambert dropped out of the scene. There's been a lot that's changed, little things that make it valid as a complete story—plus the old freedom that allows your mind to add its own interpretations."

Normally, Russell left the music to Pete, but at the end of "We're Not Gonna Take It" he wanted an angry mob in the background that boiled up to the pointed where they overthrew Tommy and smashed everything up. It took the whole of one night in the studio, plus another session, to get it right. Finally, they did it with Russell behind the microphone, goading the mob on.

It was usual to have actors in the studio, too. Nicholls was particularly impressed by Paul Nicholas, who was to play Cousin Kevin. In front of the microphone, Nicholls said, "He became a different person, he was so evil. I was watching and I felt like punching him. I thought, 'You bastard'... And then he came out and said, 'Was that all right then?' Changed back again. He did it in a couple of takes."

Oliver Reed arrived at the studio after a solid lunch with Ken Russell in an Italian restaurant. Fortunately there was more brandy in the control room.

"I sang a few notes," said Reed, "and Pete fell about."

This gave Reed the idea of playing Tommy's mother's lover Frank as burlesque. Townshend also had to coach Ann-Margret and Jack Nicholson. Their parts had to be recorded in the studio for them lip-synch to during the shooting. Daltrey, Townshend, Entwistle, Paulo Gurvitz, Jess Roden, and Billy Nicholls then laid down three- or four-part vocal harmonies to cover the actors' vocal shortcomings.

The recording took six weeks. It was hampered by a miners' strike that had cut coal stocks at power stations, causing an energy crisis that meant that businesses in Britain could only operate—and consume electricity—three days a week. Complaints by neighbors about noise meant the studio had to close at midnight, too. And the band had other commitments. They had to play several gigs in France. On May 18, they played a gig at The Valley, Charlton Athletic's soccer ground in south London. This was to have been filmed by Russell as the finale for Tommy. In the event, the B.B.C. filmed it for a fee of £800 ($1,200) and broadcast it, along with a half-hour interview with Townshend, that fall.

In June, The Who had to go over to the U.S. to play for four nights at Madison Square Garden in New York. Three of the four nights were sold out within 15 hours of a single

60-second ad broadcast at the end of special 90-minute Who edition of *The King Biscuit Flower Hour*. The band's performance was noticeably below par and there was talk of a split.

"We was fucking horrible," said Daltrey. "It just shows that we are human, though. We can have a terrible night just like everybody else."

Townshend also played his first solo gig, at the Roundhouse, in north London, during this period. He played acoustic guitar for much of the set, laying to rest his image as the mad, bad, windmilling ax man.

After the recording was done, Russell assembled a film crew of 88, mainly from people he had worked with before. Robert Stigwood had come up with £1,000,000 ($1,500,000) for the 12 weeks of scheduled shooting. In the end, the shooting took 22 weeks and cost £2,300,000 ($3,500,000).

They had a number of problems with locations. Tommy's holiday camp was built in a breaker's yard in Portsmouth, Hampshire, which specialized in decommissioning Royal Navy ships. A huge mound of buoys were painted silver to make them look like huge pinballs. These had to be repainted constantly as anyone clambering over them took the paint off with their shoes.

The weather was alternately sunny and rainy, making problems for continuity. In the "We're Not Gonna Take It" sequence Tommy finds his mother and her lover dead. Ann-Margret and Oliver Reed had to lie in a puddle in the muddy ground. Then Ann-Margret, who was known to be extremely accident prone, had to be struck over the head with a bottle. Ken Russell had two bottles made out of sugar and did the honors himself.

Daltrey, who played Tommy, also suffered in the cold and wet. He also had problems performing for the camera.

"I'd had no acting training," he said. "I was even turned down for the school play—so the fact that Tommy was deaf, dumb, and blind was a godsend."

For the "Cousin Kevin" scene, he was dunked in bath of revolting yellow liquid, then blasted with pond water from a high-pressure hose.

"This is the first and last film I make," he said. It wasn't. During the filming, it was announced that he would star as the composer in Ken Russell's next movie, *Lisztomania*. He went on to star in the movie *McVicar* in 1980 and had a considerable movie career.

Keith Moon also had a brief movie career that predated his appearance as Uncle Ernie in *Tommy*. He played "the hot nun" in Frank Zappa's 1971 movie, 200 *Motels*, and appeared with Ringo Starr, David Essex, and Billy Fury in *That'll Be The Day* in 1973. He appeared with Ringo Starr again in the 1974 comedy-horror, *Son of Dracula*, along with Harry Nilsson and Peter Frampton. Then he played J.D. Clover in the 1974 sequel to *That'll Be The Day*, called *Stardust*, with David Essex, Adam Faith, Marty Wilde, and Larry Hagman. His other movie credits were *Sonic Boom* in 1974, with Ricky Nelson, and 1978's *Sextette*, written by Mae West, in which he played a dress designer alongside Mae herself, Dom Deluise, Tony Curtis, Ringo Starr again, Alice Cooper, George Raft, Walter Pidgeon, George Hamilton, and Regis Philbin.

For Daltrey, the filming of *Tommy* would be an ordeal by fire—literally. Two rows of old pinball machines 300 feet long were stuffed with carpet underlay and soaked with kerosene. They were then set alight and, while they were burning, Daltrey had to run between them. On the third take his hair was singed and he burned his arm. Despite the injury, Townshend was impressed with the footage.

"It seemed to bring the whole thing home to me," he said. "It gives the story a stark reality I had not realized, and I personally found it staggering and very moving."

During the filming, Russell also decided that he wanted Tommy to fly, so Daltrey was sent aloft in a hang-glider. Russell assured Daltrey, who would be 400 feet up in the air, that he would perfectly safe.

"It was a bottle job, jumping off a cliff," said Daltrey. "But I would do anything for Ken."

He landed in a field of thistles.

The scene where Tommy beats the reigning pinball champion, played by Elton John, was shot in the King's Theatre in nearby Southsea. However, the local amateur dramatic society were putting on a show in the theater every night so the entire set had to be dismantled in the late afternoon, then rebuilt overnight ready to start filming again at 7.30 a.m.

In the "Pinball Wizard" scene, 1,500 extras were needed. Students from the local technical college were seconded into the movie. In payment, they were allowed to film the making of *Tommy* with equipment provided by Robert Stigwood. The Who also played a free concert for them in Portsmouth Guildhall at the end of shooting as a thank you.

While filming the scene, Ken Russell decided that Elton John's pinball machine should have a keyboard so he could play as he sang "Pinball Wizard"—while playing pinball at the same time. One of the props men ran down to the nearby Woolworth general store and bought a child's toy organ which was stuck on to the front of the machine.

The Who decided to play the accompaniment live, rather than mime to the pre-recorded backing track. During the performance, Townshend could not resist smashing his guitar to pieces. When he flung it high in the air, it came down on a girl's head, injuring her in true "Sally Simpson" style. She gushed blood and was rushed to hospital. Afterwards she told Townshend that she was "very honored" to have been hit over the head by him and he gave her the broken guitar as a memento.

Russell decided to film the "Eyesight For The Blind" sequence in a chapel dedicated to St. Marilyn—Marilyn Monroe that its. He had got the idea from filming at Lourdes, where pilgrims hope to be cured by praying to images of St. Bernadette, earlier in his career .

"Who is to say that Marilyn Monroe is less divine than Bernadette?" said Russell.

They shot the scene in a deconsecrated church in nearby Portsmouth. The local vicar complained about this and the British papers ran stories to the effect that the bearded hippie director Ken Russell was filming something amounting to an orgy on hallowed ground.

The preacher was played by Eric Clapton, who was visibly drunk. He was followed down the aisle by an uneasy-looking Pete Townshend.

"I've piddled about with acting, but I don't feel comfortable with it," said Townshend. "I do most of my acting on the typewriter."

The extras they used for this scene were genuinely blind and disabled people. Russell liked authenticity and Townshend found, when he talked to them, that they identified with Tommy, feeling normal inside but disabled outside.

"A lot of them had listened to *Tommy* and had much better credentials for getting a lift out of it than you or I," he said.

Arthur Brown was brought in to give a little extra pep to the scene, although his voice was not heard on the *Tommy* sound-track album.

In the climax of the scene, the huge Marilyn Monroe statue, in the famous pose from the 1955 movie *The Seven-Year Itch* where the air from a New York subway outlet blows up her skirt, has to fall over and smash. The props department made two Marilyns—one in glass fiber for the main shooting and one in plaster to be smashed. The glass fiber one was too big to get in though the door of the church, so it had to be made in sections and assembled inside.

The plaster one could be made inside, but was too fragile to move much, so it had to be hidden away during most of the shooting. When it was tipped over by Tommy's unseeing hand, the statue was supposed to break at the knees and smash on the floor. Instead she broke at the ankles and the high-speed camera set up to record the shot missed it. A second plaster Marilyn was made and then smashed and this time they got the shot.

All this was going on in the midst of the normal mayhem that surrounded The Who. Both Keith Moon and Oliver Reed were legendary drinkers. After a drunken binge, Reed, Moon, and Townshend found themselves marooned overnight on Townshend's new boat off Hayling Island in Hampshire when

Moon let the row boat they had taken out to it drift off. Unable to raise help with distress calls, Moon and Reed had to swim ashore to get another dinghy. They emerged naked on shore the following morning, marched straight up to the movie's catering truck and demanded brandy.

Keith Moon was enamored of Ann-Margret, too, describing her to the press as, "a lovely girl with big tits." Eric Clapton, who had just come off heroin, was also very taken with her and spent the whole of one night banging on the door of her hotel bedroom, shouting, "I'm yours Ann-Margret. I love you."

While shooting, the accident-prone Ann-Margret received a $1,000,000 settlement for a fall in a La Vegas nightclub. That same day, she was filming the scene where Tommy's mother hurls a champagne bottle through a T.V. screen and the room fills up with soap suds, then baked beans, then chocolate. During the scene, she cut her wrist on the jagged edge of the broken TV screen and was rushed to hospital where she had to have 24 stitches. Daltrey was K.O.d in the commando-training sequence and was unconscious for an hour. Perhaps fortunately, for him, a sequence where he was going to be covered in snakes was dropped when one of the snake handlers got bitten.

But the worst accident occurred when they were filming a Tommy's Holiday Camp ballroom scene on Southsea pier. A fire started and the entire wooden structure of the pier burned down. Russell filmed the event and used some of the footage in the final film.

Although much of the principal photography was done in and around Portsmouth, there was more shooting on location in Keswick in the Lake District in Cumbria and other interiors were shot in various movie studios around London.

Although Russell started out with a detailed shooting script with exact timings, on the set he improvised. He cut a whole sequence where Tommy's message is piped through a public address system, office workers leave their desk, and soldiers desert the parade ground. Instead Daltrey was to pass by and Teddy boys loafing around in the café and Hell's Angels fighting would stop, and would start dancing.

These changes sent Townshend back into the studio working seven days a week, 12 hours a day to adapt his soundtrack to the scenes Russell had shot. After that he had to take in the movie editor's final cuts.

"I went into my home studio to do four weeks of film composing on miniscule edit changes chucked at me about every hour by film editor Terry Rawlings," said Townshend.

Dubbing the soundtrack took another four months, and a number of different mixes had to be produced—mono, stereo, double stereo, and quintophonic—for the various sound systems different cinemas have. Townshend was deeply involved in this process, although mixing for a movie sound track is very different from mixing for a record.

Quintophonic sound was the forerunner of Dolby Surround Sound. It was like quadraphonic sound but had an extra speaker behind the cinema screen, so the vocals appeared to be coming from the singer. To make the quintophonic track alone took three weeks and required three mixing desks. One of them had to be place in the dead center of the dubbing theater, then as many as 50 music tracks had to be assembled. The work was so complex that

Townshend vowed never to get involved with movie sound again. Even so, he was amazed to see the results.

"It's obviously difficult for me to be objective," said Townshend, "but I remember getting a chill up my spine after seeing the rushes of the 'Acid Queen' sequence. Tina Turner is so right for the role."

Originally, Townshend had wanted Tiny Tim for the part, but Robert Stigwood had insisted on Tina Turner. But she had concert commitments in the U.S. and was on a tight schedule. She arrived in England one day, the next she recorded her track at The Who's studios, and then she spent just four days filming before returning to the U.S. Russell was famous for taking numerous takes before he was satisfied. On one occasion he made Roger Daltrey run through a field of mustard 32 times before he felt he got it right. But with Tina Turner the scenes were in the can with as few as two takes and never more than four.

The movie *Tommy* opened both sides of the Atlantic with star-studded premieres costing $100,000. At New York's Ziegfeld Theater, they had problems with the quintophonic sound system right up to the opening night, March 18. Townshend spent three hours on the day trying to adjust the delay between the back speakers and the front ones. And it was still not right when the picture began. Townshend had to leap from his seat and blunder his way in the darkness toward the sound booth to make corrections. Even so, when the movie finished, it was given a standing ovation and a number of the audience demanded that it be shown again.

Paul and Linda McCartney, Ryan and Tatum O'Neal, Tommy Smothers, and Dean Martin attended the West

Coast premiere, and the London premiere, the week after, was attended by much of the cast and other luminaries. Later the movie was shown as the closing picture at that year's Cannes Film Festival.

Tommy was now a box-office smash. In the first week of its run in the Leicester Square Theatre in London, it broke box office records, taking £26,978 ($40,500), against a previous best of £20,440 ($30,500). More money came rolling in from a range of *Tommy* merchandise—including programs, T-shirts, badges, stickers, and mirrors.

While critics raved, Russell declared in interviews that Townshend was "the new Shakespeare." However, many rock fans dismissed the movie as a bland parody of Townshend's original work. But Pete was sanguine.

"Many Who fans feel the *Tommy* film is not what The Who are about, or even what *Tommy* is about," he said. "In truth, it is exactly what it is about. It is a prime example of rock and roll throwing off its three-chord musical structure, discarding its attachment to the three-minute single, openly taking on the unfashionable questions about spirituality and religion, and yet hanging on grimly to the old ways at the same time. The *Tommy* film was the pinnacle of this gesture toward musical and verbal freedom... *Tommy* has taken his place in the established order of respectable 'safe' musical dramatic works and his heartbeat quietly throbs."

In March 1975, a soundtrack version of *Tommy* was released in the U.K. and U.S. This used reworked versions of the original songs as they appeared in the movie, plus two new songs "Champagne" and "Mother and Son" which Pete Townshend had written for Ken Russell to complete the narrative. All four members of The Who appeared on the album. However Keith Moon had moved Los Angeles and most of the drumming was done by Kenny Jones of the Small Faces. John Entwistle played the horn parts, as well as contributing most of the bass work, while Pete Townshend played synthesizer on almost every track.

Jack Nicholson and Oliver Reed could hardly sing, but their efforts were ramped by elaborate choral arrangements and backing vocalists. Ann-Margret discharged herself well and Tina Turner put in a searing version of "Acid Queen." But the highlight of the album was Elton John's version of "Pinball Wizard," with his own stage band. It was released as a single and reached number seven in the U.K. in 1975, although the single did not chart in the U.S. The album itself reached number 30 in the U.K. and number two in the U.S.

Other tracks from the soundtrack, taken from the album, or produced in other versions were also released that year, but did nothing in the charts. However, the score of the movie *Tommy* won Townshend an Oscar nomination for Best Score Adaptation. And *Tommy* was named "Best Rock Movie Or Theater Production" by the First Annual Rock Music Awards in Santa Monica, California.

The movie *Tommy* made Daltrey a huge star in America and he put out the solo album *Ride A Rock Horse*. It went to number 23 in the U.S. and 14 in the U.K. This led to new rumors that The Who were splitting up, which were further fueled by Warner Brothers who described their new movie star as "former pop star" Roger Daltrey. But Daltrey told an interviewer that he could not wait to get back on the road with "the 'orrible 'Oo—the worst rock-and-roll group in the world."

Working on the soundtrack of *Tommy* had driven Townshend to the brink of a nervous breakdown. He then wrote the powerful, painful, and self-revealing *The Who By Numbers*, which reached number seven in the U.K. and number eight in the U.S. Now 30, Townshend was gloomy and introspective, and *New Musical Express* journalist Roy Carr, who interviewed him around this time, called *The Who By Numbers* "Pete Townshend's suicide note." Townshend took himself off to the Meher Baba center in California where he was told not give up playing the guitar in The Who.

Then a financial crisis revived the band, just as it had before they created *Tommy*. They now found themselves in legal dispute with Track records and Kit Lambert, who insisted that he had written the original screenplay for *Tommy*, but had received no on-screen credit or money. The dispute froze the band's financial assets. So they had to go out on the road once more. Determined to steal the title of the "Greatest Rock Band In The World" back from the Rolling Stones, they began their new world tour in, of all places, New Bingley Hall in Stafford, a small county town 125 miles northwest of London, on October 3. Because of the success of the movie, they dropped material from their album *Quadrophenia* from the act and went back to playing on stage what they knew best—*Tommy*.

When they appeared at the Apollo theater, Glasgow, they had to go on Scottish T.V. to announce that both shows were sold out—in fact, they had received enough ticket applications to stage 14 concerts. After a few dates in Europe, they then took *Tommy* around America, kicking off at The Summit basketball arena, which had just opened in Houston,

Texas, in front of a crowd of 18,000. They set a new record at the Metropolitan Stadium in Pontiac, Michigan, drawing an audience of 78,000 and grossing $615,000. Meanwhile their new single "Squeeze Box" from *The Who By Numbers*, climbed to number 16 in the *Billboard* Hot 100 and stayed in the chart for four months. When it was released in the U.K. the following year, it went to number ten.

Keith Moon's over-literal interpretation of the lyrics of "Squeeze Box" got him arrested in Houston, Texas, although the charges were later dropped. Another incident at Prestwick airport in Scotland, where was British Airways computer was damaged, earned Moon a fine of just £65 ($100). However, as a consequence of the contretemps, airlines refused to carry the band, so they had to continue the tour by chartered jet at an estimated cost of £300,000 ($500,000).

When they returned to London that Christmas, demand for their three Christmas shows at the Hammersmith Odeon was so huge that they had to allocate tickets by lottery. Audiences went wild and critics conceded that, on stage, The Who—and *Tommy*—were back on form again. As the tour continued the following year, *Rolling Stone* magazine named them "Best Band of 1976."

They were also named the "World's Loudest Pop Group" by the *Guinness Book of Records* after a second appearance at The Valley as part of a tour of U.K. soccer grounds. Their output was measured at 120 decibels at 50 meters (166 feet). But being the World's Loudest Pop Group had its down side. Townshend was losing his hearing.

Tommy
goes marching on

When The Who produced the album *Tommy*, they alienated their old R&B fans. And when *Tommy* appeared as an all-star production and finally as a movie, more rock fans moved away from them. The huge stadium gigs that The Who were playing also had the effect of distancing them from their audience.

A general feeling of alienation of audiences from the huge stadium bands resulted in the emergence of punk rock in 1976. At that time, a band named the Sex Pistols, who came to personify U.K. punk, were playing the Marquee, where The Who had started out. Within the Pistol's early repertoire was "Substitute." At a memorable encounter in London's Speakeasy club, Sex Pistols guitarist Steve Jones and drummer Paul Cook admitted to being Who fans. Pete Townshend was soon seen as the godfather of punk, an accolade he happily accepted.

"In my imagination, I invented punk rock a thousand times," he said. It seemed to him that punk began where The Who's music left off.

But they needed the money, so touring *Tommy* around the big venues continued. This brought adulation from people who were anything but punks. When The Who played Dane County Memorial Coliseum in Madison, Wisconsin, Mayor Paul R. Soglin proclaimed an official "Who-Mania Day" and urged all music lovers, "whether or not they still have their hearing," to observe the event right throughout the city.

In September 1976, Polydor released the double album *The Story of the Who* in the U.K. It contained eight tracks from *Tommy*, had a picture of a pinball machine exploding on the sleeve, and went to number two.

In 1977, Townshend became withdrawn and the band did little. Then on September 7, 1978, Keith Moon died from a drug overdose. He was 32. The remaining members of The Who vowed to carry on. In 1979, they released the movie *The Kids Are Alright*, showing the daily life of the band—it had been filmed while Moon was still alive. The soundtrack went to number eight in the U.S. and number 26 in the U.K.

That same year, a movie version of *Quadrophenia*, based on The Who's 1973 album, was released. Townshend had little to do with the project, though Entwistle remixed the tracks for the soundtrack. Although The Who's music continued to thrill, the movie was no *Tommy*. The double album of the soundtrack went to number 46 in the U.S. and 23 in the U.K.

Also in 1979, the Rainbow version of *Tommy* took to the stage for an eight-week run in London's Queen's Theatre.

The Who kept many of the songs in their stage act because there was no end to the public's appetite for *Tommy*.

Then in 1991, 23 years after the first tracks of *Tommy* had been recorded, theater director Des McAnuff who ran a local playhouse in La Jolla, California got the idea of turning the album into a Broadway musical called *The Who's Tommy*.

"The Who's concept album *Tommy* was the first time a rock-and-roll band had created a piece of musical theater," he said. "We all created images to accompany it while we listened to *Tommy*; the music and those images combine in a powerful theater of the imagination. They were powerful enough to make me wonder why there had not been a significant stage production of *Tommy*. They made me want to talk with Pete about exploring the possibilities of a collaboration."

Townshend was enthusiastic. The idea of putting on a fully walked-through version of *Tommy* on stage had always been his dream.

"I've waited, sitting on the rights like mother hen," said Townshend, "until the public was ready to go to the legitimate theater instead of some impersonal stadium to see The Who."

There was briefly an idea that they should produce an "arenas and amphitheaters" version with Michael Hutchence of INXS as Tommy, David Bowie as Captain Walker, and Tracey Ullman as Tommy's mother. But that was soon abandoned.

"I think we realized early on that the music was the star," said McAnuff.

The cast of the musical would be the regular company members in La Jolla.

Working with McNuff, Townshend discovered new aspects of *Tommy* that he had never realized before.

"It was very strange to sit there with Des and find out I hadn't written a fantasy at all," said Townshend. "I'd written my own life story. It's a metaphor that tells the story of postwar life, and I was the child of a postwar couple. When I wrote 'See Me Feel Me,' I thought I was talking to my master [Meher Baba]. But what makes it really poignant, so wonderful, and so sublime a fragment is that it came from that place I had no control over it."

When they got down to work in La Jolla, McAnuff recalled Townshend, "striding around the room, ranting about his childhood." So in his production, instead of being a light, up-beat rock opera, *The Who's Tommy* became dark and surreal.

They spent six weeks rewriting the script. Although McAnuff took pains to remain faithful to Townshend's original concept, they found that many of Towshend's beliefs had evolved and changed.

"The spiritual metaphor I used—being deaf, dumb, and blind—equating to our spiritual ignorance, also equates to the social isolation of young people crawling out of adolescence," said Townshend. "That gave me a new way of looking at the story of *Tommy*. I was able to look at Tommy as a real person, rather than a figment of my Meher Baba-Sufi spiritual inclinations at the time."

This allowed McAnuff to develop a more hard-edged, realistic, 1990s-style production. The characterization of Tommy's parents was strengthened and the songs were reordered to make Tommy's rise to stardom seem more effortless. Like Ken Russell, McAnuff shifted the timeframe from post-World War I to post-World War II, turning the song "1921" into "1951."

"It's very much about Pete's life and times and it seemed very natural to set the story kind of post-World War II," McAnuff said.

The radical change came at the ending. Townshend had left the ending of the original nebulous and mystical. But its ambiguity had always worried him.

"You don't know whether you were supposed to side with the audience who have been used and abused and were obviously by-products of organized religion," said Townshend, "or with the benefactor, Tommy, who is the engine of it all."

In the musical's ending, Tommy and his family are reunited, in what one critic described as an "icky new feel-good finale."

In *Vanity Fair*, novelist Brett Easton Ellis called it "a Nancy Reagan ending." Townshend offered to fly to New York and punch him on the nose. As far as Townshend was concerned, McAnuff's ending in the musical was more realistic than his own in the original. After all, his parents did get back together again. He was rescued from Granny Denny and they were re-united as a family.

"What I discovered in returning to *Tommy* was that in all its vagueness, it's a story about real person and a real family," said Townshend. "I discovered that Tommy's awful neglect and traumas, the terrible abuses, the lovers, the murders—emotional murders—all of those things actually happened. They happened to me. I saw them as a young child. I saw the adult world at its worst. And I saw it at its best, because my parents finally got back together again. But I saw an ending. And so I do have an ending to *Tommy*. Which is that one forgives one's awful parents for everything they've done. Because if you don't, you'll spend the rest of your life going fucking crazy."

When his parents split, Townshend recalled, his mother's lover had wanted to take her abroad.

"My father didn't want me to go, so he took her back," said Townshend. "My mother's side of the story is that she took him back, you know, for my sake."

Having been a husband and a father himself by the time McAnuff got to work on the musical, Townshend realized that he had made just as many mistakes as his own parents had. Townshend now had tremendous sympathy for his parents' generation—the very generation that "My Generation" was rebelling against. That sympathy, he felt, came over in McAnuff's version of *Tommy*. With Tommy returning to his parents, he felt, the musical celebrated the power of the family.

"In the end the whole story turns to face God," he said. "When the people stand up and cheer, even though they may not know it, they're actually praying."

Townshend also provided another new song for the musical called "I Believe In My Own Eyes." This was designed to express Tommy's parents' frustration over Tommy as he is growing up. Townshend had been away from writing rock-and-roll songs for some time, and now, hanging around the theater, he produced a real show tune. John Entwistle said that it "sounds a bit Broadway," adding "The Who would never have done it."

The critic of the *New York Daily News* was equally scathing.

"It seems to have parachuted in from another play," he said.

As far as Townshend was concerned, he made only one stipulation concerning the production.

"No fucking dancing," he told choreographer Wayne Cilento, forcefully.

Instead there was "choreographed movement."

Spectacle was provided by video projections, flying props, and other stage effects. In "Pinball Wizard," Tommy was thrown about in a huge spinning pinball machine that bursts into flames and engulfs the whole theater in a kaleidoscope of color and light.

The Who's Tommy opened at the La Jolla Playhouse in July, 1992. Townshend, Daltrey, and Entwistle sat through the opening night, "twisting anxiously like parents at a child's first recital," according to an eye witness.

But McAnuff's high-energy production received rave reviews. The *Orange Country Register* said, "The production by La Jolla Playhouse is a visually astounding and flawlessly performed spectacle that downplays the rebellious spirit and critique of celebrity status in the original."

The *San Jose Mercury News* said, "It takes your breath away." It also spotted that the show was, "profoundly conservative... this is a parable that preaches the virtue of family."

Townshend later disputed this interpretation in *Guitar* magazine. He said that he was, "not suggesting a return to family values," but that, "the family is a fucking battlefield in which we grow up, and I think that rock and roll is about the moment we leave it and become alone."

The *San Jose Mercury News* believed the show would have a bright future.

"It looks as though the next big British rock musical to hit Broadway may come from a California theater."

In April the following year, a $6,000,000 production transferred to the St. James Theater on 44th Street, just off Broadway. *The New York Times'* theater critic Frank Rich said, "The show is not merely an entertainment juggernaut riding at full tilt on the visual and musical highs of its legendary pinball iconography and irresistible tunes, but also a surprising moving resuscitation of the disturbing passions that made *Tommy* an emblem of the era." He rued that "the authentic rock musical had eluded Broadway... until now," and said, "the show at the St. James is so theatrically fresh and emotionally raw that newcomers to *Tommy* will think it was born yesterday."

But Rich was not a newcomer to *Tommy* or The Who.

"'Hope I die before I get old,' sang The Who in 'My Generation,' its early hit single," he said, "A quarter-century or so later, Mr. Townshend hasn't got old so much as grown up into a deeper view of humanity unthinkable in the 1960s. Far from being another of Broadway's excursions into nostalgia, *The Who's Tommy* is the first musical in years to feel completely alive in its own moment. No wonder that for two hours it makes the world seem young."

Clive Barnes at the *New York Post* called *The Who's Tommy* a "blazing triumph" and said Broadway, "will never be the same again... Brilliant, bloody brilliant!" It was, another critic said, the "first fully linear *Tommy*."

By midnight the day after *The Who's Tommy*'s opening, box-office receipts totaled $494,897, beating the record set by *Guys and Dolls* one year before by $98,000. By the fifth day, it had taken $3,000,000. There was, of course, a cast recording of *The Who's Tommy*, but Townshend called in the Beatles' producer George Martin to make it.

"I love not having the responsibility," he said.

The Who's Tommy was nominated for 11 Tony Awards and won five, including Best Director. And Townshend won the Tony for Best Original Score. In his acceptance speech he said, "I saw the *Kiss Of The Spider Woman* twice and I loved it.

I saw my show 100 times and I hate it." Afterward he admitted that he was genuinely thrilled to be given the award.

"The Tony is the first artistic award I've ever had," he said. "I've never won a Grammy or anything for my creative work. At this time in my life it's like getting a knighthood."

However, the success of the new musical version of *The Who's Tommy* worried Townshend. He felt overwhelmed by his creation once more. He began drinking heavily. Backers willing to invest in new projects kept him in New York, damaging his marriage. But then in November of that year, his 1989 album *Iron Man*, based on a children's story by British poet laureate Ted Hughes, flopped, so Townshend was off the hook. He was no longer in demand. Coincidentally, McAnuff made an animated movie called *The Iron Giant* based on the same story.

The original album *Tommy* was re-mastered as a C.D., which was released in 1996. Then a deluxe 5.1 surround-sound C.D. was to be produced.

A number of stories circulated about what had happened the tapes carrying the final studio mix of *Tommy*. One was that Kit Lambert had destroyed them, so that only the "sweetened" version that was released by Decca at the time remained. But when Townshend got to work producing the surround-sound version in 2003, he found that the original stereo masters were safe and sound in the record company's vaults. For the C.D. version, Townshend worked from the original eight-track masters, so that the sound that the 21st-century listener hears is the same sound the band heard in March 1969. He also discovered a number of out-takes from the original I.B.C. session. Some of them were included on the C.D., largely to show how much fun they were having in the studio back in the fall of 1968.

The first snippet of bonus material is just 16 seconds long. Called "I Was," it is a wordless chant by The Who and whoever else happened to be in the studio at the time. Townshend provided no explanatory notes to the C.D., so it is impossible to say exactly what this puzzling fragment was for. But it is generally assumed that it was a linking piece intended to be used with either "Tommy's Holiday Camp" or "Sally Simpson."

The next is "Christmas (Out-Take 3)," which is an unused backing track for an alternate version of "Christmas." It reveals how Townshend constructs a song and shows how he, Moon, and Entwistle locked together as a musical unit when they played.

"Cousin Kevin Model Child" is the original cut from the album during the final production of the stereo master. It is mixed slightly differently to the version that appeared as a bonus track on the 1998 CD version of *Odds and Sods*.

"Young Man Blues (Version 1)" was not recorded as part of *Tommy*. It was a cover of a Mose Allison song that The Who intended to release as a stop-gap single to keep them in the charts while they were in the studio working on *Tommy*. The jazz pianist Allison had recorded this blues song on his 1957 album *Back Country Suite* on the Prestige label and it was originally called just "Blues." Daltrey *et al.* had used it in their act as The High Numbers in 1964. "Version 1" saw the light of day on Track records U.K. sampler, *The House That Track Built*, in 1969 and the song became a regular part of their stage act again. The definitive, visceral, stage version can be

heard on their 1970 album *Live At Leeds*. A slower version—
"Version 2"—can be heard on the 1998 *Odds and Sods* C.D.

Another bonus track is an alternate ensemble version of
"Tommy Can You Hear Me?"—in contrast to the acoustic
version on the original album. It has an extended end that
eventually dissolves into chaos, with Moon grunting "ooh-
ya-ooh-ya." This was the trademark of crazy British jazz
drummer Lennie Hastings.

"Trying To Get Through" was about Tommy's parents and
sung from their point of view. It was based on a riff that the
band had been playing around with on stage and in the
studio for some time. The song is not fully formed and here
they are playing around with it musically and trying to work
it up into something they can use on the album. "Keep that
going," Townshend urges as Moon slows from his usual
manic tempo. The track runs to two minutes 51 seconds here,
but the song was never finished and never made the album.

There are four minutes nine seconds of "Sally Simpson
(Out-Takes)." These consist of Townshend and Moon larking
about in an impromptu comedy routine. Damon Lyon-Shaw
announces take one, Townshend chooses the moment to
make a mock announcement to the effect that he has just
discovered—thanks to the *Record Mirror*—that his nickname
in the band is "bone." This cracks Moon up and he cackles
incessantly. This ruins the beginning of takes one through
five. Although *Tommy* has its pompous moments and the
subject matter is serious to the point of being grave, the band
believed in having fun.

"Miss Simpson" is an alternate version of "Sally Simpson."
The song here is complete, but this version lacks the

vibrancy of the track on the album. "Welcome (Take 2)" is a lifeless version of the backing track of "Welcome." There is, however, an interesting key change for the reprise of "Ask along that man who's wearing a carnation," but this was dropped from the version that made the album.

"Tommy's Holiday Camp (Band's Version)" is a full band version that is plainly designed for stage performance, but was rejected for the sparse voice and fairground-organ version found on the album.

"We're Not Gonna Take It (Alternate Version)" is the song as Townshend originally wrote it and follows his original demo. It ends with a repeat of the opening riff, followed by a final flourish. In the album version "We're Not Gonna Take It" leads into "Listening To You." This change was one of the last alterations that Townshend made to the structure of this album. So this track nearly made it on to *Tommy*.

"Dogs (Part 2)" is a jammed version of the song that appeared on the B-side of the "Pinball Wizard" single. Here, The Who sound like a garage band. With Keith Moon's frenzied drumming taking center stage, it is the nearest thing to a drum solo in The Who's catalog, although Townshend and Entwistle get their solos in too.

Tagged on at the end of the CD are five stereo-only versions of Townshend's demos—"It's A Boy," "Amazing Journey," "Christmas," "Do You Think It's Alright?," and "Pinball Wizard"—revealing more about how the original tracks were created. Interestingly, "Amazing Journey" is extended from a three-minute-41-second demo to five minutes four seconds on the album and "Christmas" goes from one minute 55 seconds to four minutes 33 seconds, while "It's A Boy" is pruned from 43 seconds to 38, "Do You Think It's Alright?" from 28 seconds to 24, and "Pinball Wizard" from three minutes 44 seconds to three minutes 17 seconds. Townshend's stereo demos have appeared on numerous bootlegs over the years and this version of "Pinball Wizard" was given away as a flexidisc with Richard Barnes' biography of The Who, *Maximum R&B*, in 1982.

appendix
The Who on tour with **Tommy**

(support acts in parentheses)

April 27, 1969: Kinema Ballroom, Dunfermline, Fife,
    Scotland.
April 28, 1969: Whitburn Bay Hotel, Sunderland.
May 1, 1969: Ronnie Scott's Jazz Club, Soho, London. An
    hour-long press preview of *Tommy*.
May 9—11, 1969: Grande Ballroom, Detroit, Michigan (Joe
    Cocker and the Grease Band).
May 13—15, 1969: The Boston Tea Party, Boston,
    Massachusetts (Roland Kirk).
May 16—18, 1969: Fillmore East, New York City, New
    York (Sweetwater, It's A Beautiful Day, and the Joshua
    Light Show).
May 19, 1969: Rock Pile Club, Toronto, Canada.
May 23 and 24, 1969: Electric Factory, Philadelphia,
    Pennsylvania.
May 25, 1969: Merriweather Post Pavilion, Columbia,
    Maryland (Led Zeppelin).
May 29—31, 1969: Kinetic Playground, Chicago, Illinois
    (Buddy Rich and the Buddy Rich Orchestra, Joe Cocker
    and the Grease Band. 31, Buddy Rich replaced by Soup).
June 1, 1969: Kiel Auditorium, St. Louis, Missouri (Joe
    Cocker and the Grease Band).

June 5 and 6, 1969: Fillmore East, New York City, New York (Chuck Berry, Albert King, and the Joshua Light Show).

June 7, 1969: Majestic Hills Theater, Lake Geneva, Wisconsin.

June 8, 1969: Tyrone Guthrie Theater, Minneapolis, Minnesota.

June 13, 1969: "Magic Circus," Hollywood Palladium, Los Angeles, California (Poco and the Bonzo Dog Doo-Dah Band).

June 17—19, 1969: Fillmore West, San Francisco, California (The Woody Herman Jazz Band).

July 5, 1969: Royal Albert Hall, Kensington Gore, London. Final night of the "Pop Proms." (Chuck Berry, Bodast).

July 19, 1969: Mothers Club, Erdington, Birmingham.

July 20, 1969: Pier Ballroom, Hastings.

July 27, 1969: The Redcar Jazz Club, Coatham Hotel, Redcar.

July 28, 1969: Fillmore North, Locarno Ballroom, Sunderland..

August 2, 1969: The Winter Garden, Eastbourne.

August 4, 1969: The Pavilion, Bath.

August 7, 1969: Assembly Hall, Worthing.

August 9, 1969: Nineth National Jazz and Blues Festival, Plumpton Racecourse, near Lewes (Chicken Shack, Yes!, The Jazz Sound of John Surman, Roy Harper, Bonzo Dog Doo-Dah Band, Aynsley Dunbar Retaliation, The Strawbs, Breakthru).

August 12, 1969: Tanglewood Music Festival, Music Shed, Tanglewood, Lenox, Massachusetts. The Who supported Jefferson Airplane (B.B. King).

August 16 and 17, 1969: Woodstock Music and Art Fair, Bethel, New York (Sly and the Family Stone).

August 22, 1969: Music Hall, Shrewsbury.

August 29, 1969: Pavilion Ballroom, Bournemouth.

August 30, 1969: Second Isle of Wight Festival of Music, Woodside Bay, Isle of Wight (Fat Mattress, Joe Cocker and the Grease Band, Bonzo Dog Doo-Dah Band, Gypsy, Marsha Hunt and White Trash, Aynsley Dunbar Retaliation, Pretty Things, Blodwyn Pig, Free, Blonde On Blonde, King Crimson).

September 6, 1969: Kinema Ballroom, Dunfermline, Fife, Scotland.

September 7, 1969: Cosmopolitan Club, Carlisle.

September 13, 1969: The Belfry, Sutton Coldfield, Birmingham.

September 21, 1969: Fairfield Hall, Croydon.

September 29, 1969: Concertgebouw, Amsterdam, Holland. *Tommy* is played in an Opera House for the first time.

October 10, 1969: Commonwealth Armory, Boston, Massachusetts (The Flock).

October 11 and 12, 1969: Grande Riviera Ballroom, Detroit, Michigan (11: Alice Cooper and The Sky, 12: All The Lonely People, and The Amboy Dukes).

October 14, 1969: CNE Coliseum, Toronto, Canada.

October 15, 1969: Capitol Theatre, Ottawa, Canada.

October 17, 1969: Holy Cross College Gymnasium, Worcester, Massachusetts (Ascension).

October 18, 1969: New York State University Gymnasium, Stony Brook, New York (The Flock).

October 19, 1969: Electric Factory, Philadelphia, Pennsylvania.

October 20—25, 1969: Fillmore East, New York City
(Joshua Light Show).

October 26, 1969: Syria Mosque, Pittsburgh, Pennsylvania
(The James Gang).

October 31, 1969: Kinetic Playground, Chicago, Illinois
(The Kinks, The Liverpool Scene).

November 1, 1969: Veterans Memorial Auditorium,
Columbus, Ohio.

November 2, 1969: McDonough Gymnasium, Georgetown
University, Washington D.C.

November 3, 1969: Westchester Country Center, White
Planes, New York.

November 4, 1969: Bushnell Auditorium, Hartford,
Connecticut.

November 6, 1969: Livingston Gymnasium, Dennison
University, Granville, Ohio.

November 7, 1969: Ohio State University, Athens, Ohio.

November 8, 1969: Kiel Opera House, St. Louis, Missouri.

November 10, 1969: Palace Theater, Albany, New York
(The Flock).

November 11 and 12, 1969: The Boston Tea Party, Boston,
Massachusetts (Tony Williams' Lifetime).

November 14, 1969: Public Music Hall, Cleveland, Ohio.

November 15, 1969: Kleinhans Music Hall, Buffalo, New
York.

November 16, 1969: Onondaga War Memorial Auditorium,
Syracuse, New York (Silk).

December 4, 1969: Hippodrome Theatre, Bristol.

December 5, 1969: Palace Theatre, Manchester.

December 12, 1969: Empire Theatre, Liverpool.

December 14, 1969: Coliseum Theatre, St. Martin's Lane, London.

December 19, 1969: City Hall, Newcastle.

January 16 and 17, 1970: Theatre des Champs Elysses, Paris, France. Start of tour of European Opera Houses.

January 24, 1970: Det Kunglige Teater, Royal Theatre, Copenhagen, Denmark.

January 26, 1970: Stadt Opernhaus, Cologne, West Germany.

January 27, 1970: Stadt Opernhaus, Hamburg, West Germany.

January 28, 1970: Stadt Opernhaus, Berlin, West Germany.

January 30, 1970: Concertgebouw, Amsterdam, Holland.

February 14, 1970: Leeds University, Leeds.

February 15, 1970: City Hall, Hull.

April 18, 1970: Leicester University, Leicester (Viv Stanshall's Big Grunt).

April 25, 1970: Nottingham University, Nottingham.

April 27, 1970: Civic Hall, Dunstable (Writing On The Wall).

May 1, 1970: Exeter University, Exeter (Mighty Baby).

May 2, 1970: Sheffield University, Sheffield.

May 8, 1970: Elliot College, University of Kent, Canterbury (Genesis).

May 9, 1970: Manchester University, Manchester.

May 15, 1970: Bailrigg University, Bailrigg, Lacashire (Quintessence).

May 16, 1970: Derwent College, University of York (Jan I Dukes De Grey).

June 7, 1970: Metropolitan Opera House, Lincoln Center, New York City, New York.

June 9 and 10, 1970: Mammoth Gardens, Denver, Colorado.

June 13, 1970: Convention Hall, Community Concourse, San Diego, California.

June 14, 1970: Anaheim Stadium, Oakland, California (Blues Image, Leon Russell, John Sebastian).

June 15 and 16, 1970: Community Theater, Berkeley, California.

June 19, 1970: Dallas Memorial Auditorium, Dallas, Texas (Cactus).

June 20, 1970: Hofheinz Pavilion, University of Houston, Houston, Texas.

June 21, 1970: Ellis Auditorium, Memphis, Tennessee.

June 22, 1970: Municipal Auditorium, Atlanta, Georgia.

June 24, 1970: The Spectrum, Philadelphia, Pennsylvania (The James Gang).

June 25 and 26, 1970: Music Hall, Cincinnati, Ohio (The James Gang).

June 27, 1970: Music Hall, Cleveland, Ohio (The James Gang, James Taylor).

June 29, 1970: Merriweather Post Pavilion, Columbia, Maryland.

July 1, 1970: Auditorium Theater, Chicago, Illinois.

July 2, 1970: Freedom Palace, Kansas City, Missouri.

July 3, 1970: Minneapolis Auditorium, Minneapolis, Minnesota.

July 4, 1970: Auditorium Theater, Chicago, Illinois.

July 5, 1970: Cobo Arena, Detroit , Michigan (The James Gang).

July 7, 1970: "Music Shed", Tanglewood, Lenox, Massachusetts (Jethro Tull, It's A Beautiful Day).

July 25, 1970: Civic Hall Dunstable (Wishbone Ash, Roger Ruskin Spear).

August 8, 1970: The Belfry, Sutton Coldfield, Birmingham.

August 24, 1970: Civic Hall, Wolverhampton (Trapeze).

August 29 and 30, 1970: Third Isle of Wight Festival of Music, East Afton Farm, near Freshwater, Isle of Wight (Cat Mother and the All Night Newsboys, Spirit, Mungo Jerry, The Doors).

September 12, 1970: Münsterland Halle, Münster, West Germany.

September 13, 1970: Oberrheinhalle, Offenbach, West Germany.

September 16, 1970: De Doelen, Rotterdam, Holland.

September 17, 1970: Concertgebouw, Amsterdam, Holland.

September 20, 1970: Falkoner Centret Teatret, Copenhagen, Denmark.

September 21, 1970: Veslby Risskov Hallen, Aarhus, Denmark.

October 6, 1970: Sophia Gardens, Cardiff, Wales (The James Gang).

October 7, 1970: Free Trade Hall, Manchester (The James Gang).

October 8, 1970: Orchid Ballroom, Purley (The James Gang).

October 10, 1970: Old Refectory, University of Sussex, Brighton (The James Gang, Roger Ruskin Spear and his Giant Kinetic Wardrobe).

October 11, 1970: Odeon Cinema, Birmingham (The James Gang).

October 13, 1970: Locarno Ballroom, Leeds (The James Gang).

October 18, 1970: Odeon Cinema, Lewisham, southeast London (The James Gang).

October 22, 1970: ABC Cinema, Stockton-on-Tees (The James Gang).

October 23, 1970: Green's Playhouse, Glasgow, Scotland (The James Gang).

October 24, 1970: Sheffield University, Sheffield (The James Gang).

October 25, 1970: Empire Theatre, Liverpool (The James Gang).

October 26, 1970: Trentham Gardens, Stoke-on-Trent (The James Gang).

October 29, 1970: Palais, Hammersmith, London (Roger Rushkin Spear and his Giant Kinetic Wardrode).

November 21, 1970: Leeds University, Leeds.

November 26, 1970: Fillmore North, Mayfair Ballroom, Newcastle (Curved Air).

November 28, 1970: Lanchester College, Coventry.

December 5, 1970: The Lad's Club, Norwich.

December 15, 1970: Mayfair Ballroom, Newcastle.

December 16, 1970: Futurist Theatre, Scarborough, Yorkshire.

December 20, 1970: The Roundhouse, London. "Implosion" show (America, Patta, Chalk Farm District Salvation Army—carol singing, Elton John).

February 14 and 15, 1971: *Lifehouse* Concert, Young Vic Theatre, Waterloo, southeast London.

February 20, 1971: *Lifehouse* Concert, Young Vic Theatre, Waterloo, southeast London.

February 22, 1971: *Lifehouse* Concert, Young Vic Theatre, Waterloo, southeast London.

March 1, 1971: *Lifehouse* Concert, Young Vic Theatre, Waterloo, southeast London.

April 2, 1971: A ballet adaptation of *Tommy*, by the Montreal-based "Les Grands Ballets Canadiens", opens at the City Center Theater, New York City, for a fort night's run. There was further run in October.

April 26, 1971: *Lifehouse* Concert, Young Vic Theatre, Waterloo, southeast London.

April 28, 1971: A new musical interpretation of *Tommy* was staged by the Seattle Opera Company at The Moore Theater, Seattle, Washington. It ran for three weeks.

May 5, 1971: The final *Lifehouse* Concert, Young Vic Theatre, Waterloo, southeast London.

May 7, 1971: "Fillmore North", Top Rank Suite, Sunderland. The first in a series of "secret" shows.

May 13, 1971: Kinetic Circus, Mayfair Suite, Birmingham.

May 14, 1971; Liverpool University, Liverpool.

May 23, 1971: Caird Hall, Dundee, Tayside, Scotland.

June 26, 1971: Reading Festival, Reading.

July 1, 1971: Assembly Hall, Worthing.

July 3, 1971: City Hall, Sheffield.

July 4, 1971: De Monfort Hall, Leicester.

July 8, 1971: The Pavilion, Bath.

July 10, 1971: Civic Hall, Dunstable.

July 12, 1971: The Winter Garden, Eastbourne.

July 15, 1971: Tow Hall, Watford.

July 29 and 31, 1971: Forest Hills Music Festival, Forest Hills Tennis Stadium, Forest Hills, New York City, New York (Patti LaBelle).

August 2, 1971: Center For The Performing Arts, Saratoga Springs, New York (Patti LaBelle).

August 3, 1971: The Spectrum, Philadelphia, Pennsylvania (Patti LaBelle).

August 4—7, 1971: Music Hall, Boston Massachusetts (4, 5 Mylon, 6, 7 Patti LaBelle).

August 9, 1971: War Memorial Auditorium, Rochester, New York (Patti LaBelle).

August 10, 1971: Civic Arena, Pittsburgh, Pennsylvania (Patti LaBelle).

August 12, 1971: Public Music Hall, Cleveland, Ohio (Patti LaBelle).

August 13, 1971: O'Hara Arena, Dayton, Ohio (Patti LaBelle).

August 14, 1971: Cobo Arena, Detroit, Michigan (Patti LaBelle).

August 15, 1971: Metropolitan Sports Center, Minneapolis, Minnesota (Patti LaBelle).

August 16, 1971: Mississippi River Festival, Edwardsville Campus, Southern Illinois University, Edwardsville, Illinois.

August 17—19, 1971: Auditorium Theater, Chicago, Illinois (Patti LaBelle).

September 18, 1971: The Oval Cricket Ground, Kennington, southeast London. "Goodbye Summer" charity concert (Cochise, The Grease Band, Lindisfarne, Quintessence, Mott the Hoople, America, Eugene Wallace, Atomic Rooster, The Faces).

September 28, 1971: Free Trade Hall, Manchester.

October 2, 1971: Reading University, Reading (Ron Geesin).

October 9, 1971: University of Surrey, Guildford, Surrey (Ron Geesin).

October 10, 1971: Elliot College, University of Canterbury, Canterbury (Ron Geesin).

October 18, 1971: Guildhall, Southampton (Quiver).

October 20, 1971: Odeon Theatre, Birmingham (Quiver).

October 21, 1971: Green's Playhouse, Glasgow, Scotland (Quiver).

October 22, 1971: Opera House, Blackpool (Quiver).

October 23, 1971: Liverpool University, Liverpool (Quiver).

October 24, 1971: Trentham Gardens, Stoke-on-Trent (Quiver).

October 28, 1971: Odeon Cinema, Manchester (Quiver).

October 30, 1971: Odeon Cinema, Newcastle (Quiver).

November 4—6, 1971: Rainbow Theatre, Finsbury Park, north London (Quiver).

November 9, 1971: Green's Playhouse, Glasgow (Quiver).

November 20, 1971: Charlotte Coliseum, Charlotte, North Carolina (Bell and Arc).

November 22, 1971: University of Alabama Memorial Coliseum, Tuscaloosa, Alabama (Bell and Arc).

November 23, 1971: Municipal Auditorium, Atlanta, Georgia (Bell and Arc).

November 25 and 26, 1971: Miami Beach Convention Hall, Miami, Florida (Bell and Arc).

November 28, 1971: Mid-South Coliseum, Memphis, Tennessee (Bell and Arc).

November 29 and 30, 1971: The Warehouse, New Orleans, Louisiana (Bell and Arc).

December 1, 1971: Sam Houston Coliseum, Houston, Texas (Bell and Arc).

December 2, 1971: Dallas Memorial Auditorium, Dallas, Texas (Bell and Arc).

December 4 and 5, 1971: Denver Coliseum, Denver, Colorado (Mylon Le Fevre, Holy Smoke).

December 7, 1971: Veterans Memorial Coliseum, Phoenix, Arizona (Mylon Le Fevre Holy Smoke).

December 8, 1971: San Diego Sports Arena, San Diego, California (Mylon Le Fevre, Holy Smoke).

December 9, 1971: Inglewood Forum, Los Angeles, California (Mylon Le Fevre, Holy Smoke).

December 10, 1971: Civic Arena, Long Beach, California (Mylon Le Fevre, Holy Smoke).

December 12 and 13, 1971: Civic Auditorium, San Francisco, California (Mylon Le Fevre, Holy Smoke).

December 15, 1971: Center Coliseum, Seattle, Washington (Mylon Le Fevre, Holy Smoke).

February 22, 1972: Joel Rosensweig's production of *Tommy* opened at the Aquarius Theater, Sunset and Vine, Hollywood, California. It ran through to March 26.

August 11, 1972: Festhall, Frankfurt, West Germany (Golden Earring).

August 12, 1972: Ernst Merck Halle, Hamburg, West Germany (Golden Earring).

August 16, 1972: Forest Nationale, Brussels, Belgium (Golden Earring).

August 17, 1972: Oude Rai, Amsterdam, Holland (Golden Earring).

August 21, 1972: KB Hallen, Copenhagen, Denmark (Golden Earring).

August 23, 1972: Kungliga Tennishallen, Stockholm, Sweden (Golden Earring).

August 24, 1972: Scandinavium, Gothenburg, Sweden (Golden Earring).

August 25, 1972: KB Hallen, Copenhagen, Denmark (Golden Earring).

August 30, 1972: Deutschlandhalle, Berlin, West Germany (Golden Earring).

August 31, 1972: Grughalle, Essen, West Germany (Golden Earring).

September 2, 1972: Stadhalle, Vienna, Austria (Golden Earring).

September 4, 1972: Deutsches Museum, Kongressaal, Munich, West Germany (Golden Earring).

September 5, 1972: Mehrzweckhalle, Wetzikon, Zurich, Switzerland (Golden Earring).

September 9, 1972: Fête de L'Humanité (French Worker Festival), Paris, France (Country Joe McDonald).

September 10, 1972: Palais des Sports, Lyon, France (Golden Earring).

September 14, 1972: Palasport, Rome, Italy (Golden Earring).

December 9, 1972: Two sell-out shows of Lou Reizner's production of *Tommy*, Rainbow Theatre, Finsbury Park, London. Performed by the band with The London Symphony Orchestra and The English Chamber Choir.

March 10, 1973: De Vliegermolen Sportshal, Voorburg, The Hague, Holland. "Popgala" (The Faces, Rory Gallagher, Gary Glitter).

October 28, 1973: Trentham Gardens, Stoke-on-Trent.

October 29, 1973: Civic Hall, Wolverhampton.

November 1 and 2, 1973: King's Hall, Belle Vue,
Manchester (Kilburn and the High Roads).

November 5—7, 1973: Odeon Theatre, Newcastle (Kilburn
and the High Roads).

November 11—13, 1973: Lyceum Theatre, London
(Kilburn and the High Roads).

November 20, 1973: Cow Palace, San Francisco, California
(Lynyrd Skynyrd).

November 22 and 23, 1973: Inglewood Forum, Los
Angeles, California (Lynyrd Skynyrd).

November 25, 1973: Dallas Memorial Auditorium, Dallas,
Texas (Lynyrd Skynyrd.

November 27, 1973: The Omni, Atlanta, Georgia (Lynyrd
Skynyrd).

November 28, 1973: St. Louis Arena, St. Louis, Missouri
(Lynyrd Skynyrd).

November 29, 1973: International Ampitheater, Chicago,
Illinois (Lynyrd Skynyrd).

November 30, 1973: Cobo Arena, Detroit Michigan
(Lynyrd Skynyrd).

December 2, 1973: The Forum, Montreal, Canada (Lynyrd
Skynyrd).

December 3, 1973: Boston Garden, Boston, Massachusetts
(Lynyrd Skynyrd).

December 4, 1973: The Spectrum, Philadelphia,
Pennsylvania (Lynyrd Skynyrd).

December 6, 1973: Capital Center, Largo, Maryland
(Lynyrd Skynyrd).

December 18 and 19, 22 and 23: Sundown Theatre, Edmonton, north London.

February 9, 1974: Palais des Grottes, Cambrai, Lille, France (John "Speedy" Keene and band).)

February 10, 1974: Parc des Expositions, Paris, France (John "Speedy" Keene and band.

February 15, 1974: Palais des Sports Armes, Poitiers, France (John "Speedy" Keene and band).

February 17, 1974: Foire de Toulouse, Toulouse, France (John "Speedy" Keene and band).

February 22, 1974: Parc des Expositions, Nancy, France (John "Speedy" Keene and band).

February 24, 1974: Palais des Sports, Lyon, France (John "Speedy" Keene and band).

May 6, 1974: New Theatre, Oxford.

May 18, 1974: "Summer of '74" concert, Charlton Athletic Football Ground, The Valley, southeast London (Lou Reed, Humble Pie, Bad Company, Lindisfarne, Montrose, Maggie Bell).

May 22, 1974: Guildhall, Portsmouth. A private "thank you" concert for the student extras who worked on the film version of *Tommy* (Gypsy).

March 18, 1975: World premiere of *Tommy The Movie* at Ziegfeld Theater, New York City.

October 3 and 5, 1975: New Bingley Hall, Stafford County Showground, Staffordshire.

October 6 and 7, 1975: King's Hall, Belle Vue, Manchester.

October 15 and 16, 1975: Apollo, Glasgow, Scotland.

October 18 and 19, 1975: Granby Halls, Leicester.

October 21, 23 and 24, 1975: Empire Pool, Wembley, London.

October 27, 1975: The Ahoy, Rotterdam, Holland.

October 28, 1975: Stadthalle, Vienna, Austria.

October 29, 1975: Stadthalle, Bremen, West Germany

October 30 and 31, 1975: Philipshalle, Düsseldorf, West Germany.

November 2 and 3, 1975: Messehalle, Sindelfingen, West Germany.

November 6 and 7, 1975: Eherhalle, Ludwigshafen, West Germany

November 20, 1975: The Summit, Houston, Texas (Toots and the Maytals).

November 21, 1975: L.S.U. Assembly Center, Baton Rouge, Louisiana (Toots and the Maytals).

November 23, 1975: Mid-South Coliseum, Memphis, Tennessee (Toots and the Maytals).

November 24, 1975: The Omni, Atlanta, Georgia (Toots and the Maytals).

November 25, 1975: M.T.S.U. Murphy Center, Murfreesboro, Tennessee (Toots and the Maytals).

November 27, 1975: Hampton Coliseum, Hampton Roads, Virginia (Toots and the Maytals).

November 28, 1975: Coliseum, Greensboro, North Carolina (Toots and the Maytals).

November 30, 1975: Indiana University Assembly Hall, Bloomington, Indiana (Toots and the Maytals).

December 1, 1975: Kemper Arena, Kansas City, Missouri (Toots and the Maytals).

Dececmber 2, 1975: Veterans Memorial Auditorium, Des Moines, Iowa (Toots and the Maytals).

December 4 and 5, 1975: Chicago Stadium, Chicago, Illinois (Toots and the Maytals).

December 6, 1975: Metropolitan Stadium, Pontiac, Michigan (Toots and the Maytals).

December 8, 1975: Riverfront Coliseum, Cincinnati, Ohio (Toots and the Maytals).

December 9, 1975: Richfield Coliseum, Cleveland, Ohio (Toots and the Maytals).

December 10, 1975: Memorial Auditorium, Buffalo, New York (Toots and the Maytals).

December 11, 1975: Maple Leaf Garden, Toronto,Canada (Toots and the Maytals).

December 13, 1975: Civic Center, Providence, Rhode Island (Toots and the Maytals).

December 14, 1975: Civic Center, Springfield, Massachusetts (Toots and the Maytals).

December 15, 1975: The Spectrum, Philadelphia, Pennsylvania (Toots and the Maytals).

December 21—23, 1975: Hammersmith Odeon, Hammersmith, London.

February 27, 1976: Hallenstadion, Zurich, Switzerland (The Steve Gibbons Band).

February 28, 1976: Oympiahalle, Munich, West Germany.

March 1 and 2, 1976: Pavilion de Paris, Paris, France.

March 9, 1976: Boston Gardens, Boston, Massachusetts (The Steve Gibbons Band).

March 11, 1976: Madison Square Garden, New York City, New York (The Steve Gibbons Band).

March 13, 1976: Dane County Memorial Coliseum, Madison, Wisconsin (The Steve Gibbons Band).

March 14, 1976: Civic Center Arena, St. Paul, Minnesota
(The Steve Gibbons Band).

March 15, 1976: Myraid Convention Center, Oklahoma
City, Oklahoma (The Steve Gibbons Band).

March 16, 1976: Tarrant County Convention Center, Fort
Worth, Texas (The Steve Gibbons Band).

March 18, 1976: Salt Palace Convention Center, Salt Lake
City, Utah (The Steve Gibbons Band).

March 21, 1976: Anaheim Stadium, Anaheim, California
(Steve Gibbons Band, Little Feat, Rufus and Chaka Khan).

March 24, 1976: Memorial Coliseum, Portland, Oregon
(The Steve Gibbons Band).

March 25, 1976: Seattle Center Coliseum, Seattle,
Washington (The Steve Gibbons Band).

March 27 and 28, 1976: Winterland, San Francisco,
California (The Steve Gibbons Band).

March 30, 1976: McNichols Sports Arena, Denver,
Colorado (The Steve Gibbons Band).

April 1, 1976: Boston Garden, Boston, Massachusetts (The
Steve Gibbons Band).

May 22, 1976: Parc des Expositions, Colmar, France.

May 25, 1976: Palais des Sports, Lyon, France.

May 31, 1976: Charlton Athletic Football Ground, The
Valley, southeast London. "Who Put The Boot In" show
(Widowmaker, The Outlaws, Chapman-Whitney's
Streetwalkers, Little Feat, Sensational Alex Harvey Band).

June 5, 1976: Celtic Football Club, Celtic Park, Glasgow,
Scotland. "Who Put The Boot In" show (Widowmaker,
The Outlaws, Chapman-Whitney's Streetwalkers, Little
Feat, The Sensational Alex Harvey Band).

June 12, 1976: Swansea City Football Club, Vetch Field, Swansea, Wales. "Who Put The Boot In" show (Widowmaker, Outlaws, Chapman-Whitney's Streetwalkers, Little Feat, The Sensational Alex Harvey Band).

August 3 and 4, 1976: Capital Center, Largo, Maryland (Law).

August 7, 1976: Gator Bowl, Jacksonville, Florida (Law, Black Oak Arkansas, Patti LaBelle).

August 9, 1976: Miami Basketball Stadium, Miami, Florida (Law, The Outlaws, Montrose).

October 6, 1976: Veterans Memorial Coliseum, Phoenix, Arizona.

October 7, 1976: Sports Arena, San Diego, Calif.

October 9 and 10, 1976: Alameda County Stadium, Oakland, California. "Day On The Green" show (The Grateful Dead).

October 13, 1976: Memorial Coliseum, Portland, Oregon.

October 14, 1976: Center Coliseum, Seattle, Washington.

October 16, 1976: Northlands Coliseum, Edmonton, Canada.

October 18, 1976: Winnipeg Arena, Winnipeg, Canada.

October 21, 1976: Maple Leaf Gardens, Toronto, Canada.

Tommy **revival dates**

September 10 and 11, 1982: N.E.C, Birmingham.

September 22 and 23, 1982: Capital Center, Landover, Maryland.

September 25, 1982: JFK Stadium, Philadelphia, Penn.

September 26, 1982: Rich Stadium, Buffalo, New York.

September 28, 1982: Civic Center, Pittsburgh, Penn.

September 29, 1982: Market Square Arena, Indianapolis, Indiana.

September 30, 1982: Silverdome, Pontiac, Michigan

October 2 and 3, 1982: Civic Center, St. Paul, Minnesota.

October 5 and 6, 1982: Rosemont Horizon, Chicago, Illinois.

October 7, 1982: Freedom Hall, Louisville, Kentucky.

October 9, 1982: Exhibition Stadium, Toronto, Canada.

October 10, 1982: Brendan Byrne Arena, East Rutherford, NJ.

October 12 and 13, 1982: Shea Stadium, New York, NY.

October 15, 1982: Uni Dome, Cedar Falls, Iowa.

October 17, 1982: Folsum Fields, Boulder, Colorado.

October 20, 1982: Kingdome, Seattle, Washington.

October 21, 1982: Portland Coliseum, Portland, Oregon.

October 23, 1982: Oakland Stadium, Oakland, California.

October 25, 1982: Oakland Coliseum, Oakland, California.

October 27, 1982: Jack Murphy Stadium, San Diego, Calif.

October 29, 1982: Memorial Coliseum, Los Angeles, Calif.

October 31, 1982: Sun Devil Stadium, Phoenix, Arizona.

November 27, 1982: Tangerine Bowl, Orlando, Florida.

November 29, 1982: Rupp Arena, Lexington, Kentucky.

November 30, 1982: Civic Arena, Birmingham, Alabama.

December 1, 1982: Coast Coliseum, Biloxi, Mississippi.

December 3,1982: were scheduled to play at The Astrodome, Houston, Texas.

Full cast and crew for Tommy (1975)

Directed by Ken Russell

Writing credits:
Pete Townshend (album)
Ken Russell (screen play)

Cast (in credits order) verified as complete:

Oliver Reed	Frank Hobbs
Ann-Margret	Nora Walker Hobbs
Roger Daltrey	Tommy Walker
Elton John	Pinball Wizard
Eric Clapton	Preacher
John Entwistle	Himself
Keith Moon	Uncle Ernie
Paul Nicholas	Cousin Kevin
Jack Nicholson	A Quackson (mental health specialist)
Robert Powell	Group Captain Walker
Pete Townshend	Himself
Tina Turner	The Acid Queen
Arthur Brown	The priest
Victoria Russell	Sally Simpson
Ben Aris	Rev. A. Simpson V.C.
Mary Holland	Mrs Simpson
Gary Rich	Rock musician
Dick Allan	President Black Angels

Barry Winch	Young Tommy
Eddie Stacey	Bovver boy
Liza Strike	Vocal chorus (voice)
Simon Townshend	Newsboy/Vocal chorus
Mylon LeFevre	Vocal chorus (voice)
Billy Nicholls	Vocal chorus (voice)
Jeff Roden	Vocal chorus (voice)
Margo Newman	Nurse number 1/Vocal chorus (voice)
Gillian McIntosh	Vocal chorus (voice)
Vicki Brown	Nurse number 2/Vocal chorus (voice)
Kit Trevor	Vocal chorus (voice)
Helen Shappel	Vocal chorus (voice)
Paul Gurvitz	Vocal chorus (voice)
Alison Dowling	Young Tommy/Vocal chorus (voice)

Rest of cast listed alphabetically:

Jennifer Baker	Nurse number 1 (uncredited)
Susan Baker	Nurse number 2 (uncredited)
Imogen Claire	Nurse at the specialist's practice (uncredited)
Christine Hewett	Lady in Black Beauty chocolate commercial (uncredited)
Juliet King	Handmaiden to the Acid Queen (uncredited)
Gillian Lefkowitz	Handmaiden to the Acid Queen (uncredited)
Ken Russell	(cameo, uncredited)

select bibliography

Atkins, John, *The Who on Record – A Critical History*, 1963-1998, McFarland & Company, Jefferson, North Carolina, 2000

Barnes, Richard and Townshend, Pete, *The Story of Tommy*, Eel Pie Publishing, Twickenham, Middlesex, 1977

Barnes, Richard, *The Who: Maximum R & B: A Visual History*, Eel Pie Publishing, Twickenham, Middlesex, 1982

Bogovich, Richard, *The Who's Who*, McFarland & Company, Jefferson, North Carolina, 2002

Butler, Dougal, *Full Moon: The Amazing Rock and Roll Life of the Late Keith Moon*, William Morrow & Co, New York, 1981

Butler, Dougal, *Moon the Loon*, Star Books, London,1981

Charlesworth, Chris, *The Complete Guide to the Music of The Who*, Ominbus Press, London, 1995

DeCurtis, Anthony and Henke, James, *The Rolling Stone Illustrated History of Rock and Roll*, Plexus, London,1992

Ewbank, Tim and Hildred, Stafford, *Roger Daltrey: The Biography*, Portrait, London, 2004

Fletcher, Tony, *Dear Boy: The Life of Keith Moon*, Omnibus, London, 1998

Giuliano, Geoffrey, *Behind Blue Eyes—A Life of Pete Townshend*, Hodder & Stoughton, London, 1996

Goddard, Peter and Kamin, Philip, *The Who—The Farewell Tour*, Sidgwick & Jackson, London, 1983

Hanel, Ed, *The Illustrated Discography*, Omnibus Press, London, 1981

Herman, Gary, *The Who*, Studio Vista, London, 1971

Hesse, Hermann, *Siddhartha*, Shambhala, Boston, 2002

Neil, Andy and Kent, Matt, *Anyway Anyhow Anywhere—The Complete Chronicle of The Who, 1958-1978*, Virgin Books, London, 2002

Perry, John, *The Who—Meaty Beaty Big and Bouncy*, Schirmer Books, New York, 1998

Smith, Larry David, *Pete Townshend—The Minstrel's Dilemma*, Praeger, Westport, Connecticut, 1999

Sydow, Karl, *Bass Culture: The John Entwistle Guitar Collection*, Sanctuary, London, 2004

Townshend, Pete and McAnuff, Des, *The Who's Tommy: The Musical*, Pantheon, London, 1993

Townshend, Pete, *Tommy: the Musical.* Vintage, London, 1999

Waterman, Ivan, *Keith Moon: The Life and Death of a Rock Legend*, Arrow Books, London, 1979

Wharton, Gary, *Chasing the Wind: A Quadrophenia Anthology*, Lushington, Cardiff, 2002

Who, The, *A Decade of The Who,*. Fabulous Music Ltd, London, 1977

Wolter, Stephen and Kimber, Karen, *The Who in Print—An Annotated Bibliography, 1965 through 1990*, McFarland & Company, Jefferson, North Carolina, 1992

index

222